Praise God

I'm Free!

Second Edition

Inspirational Short Stories and Poems on God's Perception of Human Identity

MONIQUE R. FOSTER

PRAISE GOD I'M FREE!
SECOND EDITION

© 2016 Monique Foster
ISBN 13: 978-0-9971929-0-2

All rights reserved.
No part of this publication may be reproduced, stored in a retrieval system, or transmitted in any form or by any means, electronic, mechanical, photocopying, recording or otherwise, without the prior permission of the publisher. Permission to reproduce in any part, must be obtained in writing.

Unless otherwise noted, all scripture taken from the King James Version. Used by permission. All rights reserved.
Scripture quotations marked (AMP) are taken from the Amplified Bible, Copyright © 1954, 1958, 1962, 1964, 1965, 1987 by The Lockman Foundation. Used by permission.

For speaking engagements and information, please contact:
Monique Foster
Moniquefoster1972@gmail.com

Published by Dream Birthers LLC
www.DreamBirthers.com

Congratulations to my sister-in-law Monique!

After a review of this book, "Praise God I'm Free," I reflect on the gracious chapters. How pleased I am with the pleasant and forward transparency of integrity of this book! It is like reading a smorgasbord of many tasty different items that express the adventure of a righteous mind, no doubt it relays with décor the mind of one who has gladly embraced the issues of life with God's inspiration! I'm sure that the ones who read this book will find it encouraging, personal, personally, consoling, relational and enduring as one of those articles that people would like to read again and again!... A goodly read indeed! Simply put… A very pleasant book it is!

Be Blessed!!!

Daniel Foster, CEO: Flywheel Ministries Press

Chairman: Writers, Publishers, Media Group (WPM Group)

Author: The Toll Road Series and The Land of Proveenia

Endorsement for, I Will Praise Thee for I am Fearfully and Wonderfully Made by Monique Foster

The title of the book says it all – I Praise You Lord God because You made me so wonderfully. As I read each story, I am forever persuaded that God's love is awesome and that His healing power is real and sustaining. No matter what you have experienced in life, God heals and helps you get the treasure that's inside you – out. Each and every story, poem and musing speaks to how real God is and it makes me want to praise Him. Read this treasure.

Rose M. Smith

TABLE OF CONTENTS

AUTHOR'S NOTE 11
IDENTITY 17
    I WILL PRAISE THEE FOR I AM FEARFULLY AND WONDERFULLY MADE 19
    YOU ARE FEARFULLY AND WONDERFULLY MADE 20
    THIS LOVE IS REAL 22
    THE HEART OF GOD IS FULL FOR EVERYONE 24
    OUR TRUST IS IN YOU 25
    MEET ME BEHIND THE VEIL 28
    CHAMPION OF FAITH 31
    BROKEN BUT NOT TORN APART 33
    YOU ARE AN OVERCOMER FROM BIRTH 35
    MY ATTITUDE IS MY ALTITUDE 37
    MEND WHAT IS BROKEN, "LORD TAKE THIS HEART OF MINE AND FIX IT." 40
    SOLDIER YOU ARE 42
    MY BEST FRIEND 44
    MAN!!! 46
    IF I WERE YOUR QUEEN 47
    OWE NO ONE AN APOLOGY FOR WHO GOD HAS CREATED YOU TO BE 49
    GOD'S EYES 52
    MANY FACES OF ME 53
    PRAISE IS YOUR WEAPON 56
    YOU CAN NEVER COME IN BETWEEN A GIRL AND HER MUSIC COME

    on Let's Dance! 59
    Bitter, Battered, Black and Wounded 61
    Hand Me Another Brick 64
    I Want To Be More Than Just A Trophy On Your Side! 66
    A Humble Heart Will Always…… 68
    A Heart Of Stone! 70
    Genetics 72

Family 75
    Jealousy 77
    Momma and Daddy's Eyes 79
    Grandma's Angel 81
    Switchin' in the Kitchen 83
    The Silent Whispers Will Always Be Cherished 84
    A Little Boy Who Never Listens 85
    Big Brother 87
    Sisterly Love 90
    Mama's Kitchen 92
    I've Seen The Tears You Shed 94
    I Have A Momma Who Are You? 95

Society 97
    Who Am I? 99
    My Best Friend… 101
    Don't Judge Me 103
    If I Were the President for a Year 105
    Like a Whirlwind 107
    Set Me Free! 110
    Press Through Your Distractions 112

GOSSIP	113
WHO OFFENDED YOU?	116
GOD GIVE ME A MILLION SO I CAN BE FREE!	118
WHY HAVE YOU MADE ME YOUR ENEMY?	119
I'M JUST A NEGRA AS YOU?	120
AMERICA THE HOME OF THE FREE	122
CAN I BE JUST AN AMERICAN AS YOU?	124
POWER!	126
DON'T WEAKEN ME SO YOU CAN BE STRONG!	129
ATTACK	131
HEARTLESS PEOPLE DO HEARTLESS THINGS	132
A DESPERATE CRY FOR HELP!	133
GET RID OF ME SET ME FREE!	135
I AM NOT YOUR PUNCHING BAG I AM NOT YOUR EXCUSE!	138
BEAT HER MASTER IT WASN'T ME!	140
SET MY PEOPLE FREE!	141
DON'T!	143
IT'S NOT A FIGMENT OF OUR IMAGINATION	145
I'M READY	147
LET ME INTRODUCE YOU TO MY COUNSELOR	148
ALL MY LIFE I HAD TO FIGHT!	149
DREAMS AND VISIONS	**152**
A STAR FOR THE DAY	154
IN MY EYES	155
HEAVEN ON EARTH	157
I'M A GO GETTER, NOT A GOLD DIGGER	160
MY DESIRE	161

A MAN THAT CAN PRAISE GOD IS A KEEPER	162
EMBRACE ME AGAIN	164
THE PERFECT ME	166
THE DEW IN THE MORNING REST FRESH UPON MY HEART	167
CAN'T NOBODY STEAL MY DREAM!	168
IF YOU DON'T LIVE FOR WHAT YOU BELIEVE …	171
KEEP ME AND LET ME FLY!	172
I WANT MY OWN ISLAND	173
HIDE MY EMOTIONS SO THAT I CAN SEE	175
YOU HAVE THE POWER TO CHANGE YOUR STORY…	177
BATTLEFIELD OF THE MIND	180
WHAT DO YOU DO WHEN…	181
IS MY BLACK NOT BLACK ENOUGH FOR YOU?	184
YOU'RE A VERY SPECIAL…IN THE GREAT GOD'S KINGDOM WORLD	186
ACKNOWLEDGMENTS	188

AUTHOR'S NOTE
(A Reflection from Robert Frost's poem, The Road Not Taken)

Have you ever come to the fork in the road, where you had to make a decision as to what path to go down? Why is it that the path that looks greener seemed to be the longer road to take? It was prettier and it looked more enjoyable. Some people took that longer road and some took the shorter, because they felt either it was a better path or shorter distance to their destiny.

The shorter path was the harder for me. Even if the greener seemed to look better, it looked like it would take too long to reach my destiny. I also felt I could not go down this road because I thought I was not good enough. That is what I was told by other influencers in my life. I always dreamed and probably attempted to go down the better path for success, for riches, and achievements, everyone wants to be like the Jones's, right? There had to be an inner strength for me to believe. It had to be God's grace to get me there!

I believe it was in the year of 2002-2003 when there was a fork in the road planted for me. I was a single mother working very hard to provide for her daughter. I was working in the corporate world and it was a great struggle because of corporate political reasons and not knowing my self-worth or identity. I had two things against me, I **was** a single black woman, who held no college degree. I held several certifications of completion in professional development schools, but it was never honored. I was always the one to encourage others in their journey but I couldn't see myself down that same road of success. I really didn't have the confidence because it was torn down by my competitors.

Not only did I struggle with my confidence in the career of choice. I struggled in my spiritual walk with my Lord and Savior Jesus Christ. Every relationship I had was incomplete and broken, that would include family, friends, my relationship with God, career, and etc. In my eyes, there was really no hope for marriage. I wanted so badly to make something out of nothing on my own but, the only one to do it had to be God the Father, God the Son, and God the Holy Spirit. No one else could make me whole. I was at times desperate and had little faith but, I still had great dreams.

Always being compared to the other women, never knowing my true identity and self-worth, being cornered and bullied trying to fight my way out. I had to one day say enough is enough! There was a desperate war cry that came out of me. In fear and torment, I ran to the right place, a church where the chaos wasn't so loud. God wanted to mature me in ways that I never knew. It was time to grow up!

I went to a church service one day and my ears finally opened to what God's word said about my life. The man of God quoted the scripture in Psalm 139:14 "I will praise thee for I am fearfully and wonderfully made: Marvelous are thy works; and that my soul knoweth right well. I would consider myself to be one who was semi-pretty and acceptable but because of low self-esteem, I let Satan drag me into a place of insecurity and neglect. This one word rang in my ears for several years before it had to take root and grow because of the unknown.

After, repenting to God, and others, I had to go down the road of healing and deliverance. This road God allowed me to become whole with receiving his spirit. Years went by and I thought I was just doing things right by just being obedient, being faithful in going to church, singing in the choir and on the praise and worship team, and reading his Word. Yet, there was more He had for me to do. He wanted my whole heart. David said, "With my whole heart have I sought thee: O let me not wander from thy commandments." (Psalms 119:10, KJV) That's when I finally was able to experience the Lord my God.

My church, at the time, was going through a series of studies about miracles, signs, and wonders. My pastor, Pastor Willie Powell, spoke a sermon to the single women about making a request known unto God and he very explicitly told us to, "Write the vision, and make it plain upon the table, that he may run the readeth it. For the vision is yet for an appointed time…" (Habakkuk 2:3). At the time, I had BIG Faith. I thought God to be the GOD of the impossible as he was in my life. Some people may say that Pastor Powell was brain washing us. I will say he was just being the obedient servant of God that he is today by declaring the word of God to be true.

Habakkuk 2:3, was a familiar Chapter to me that was spoken by another leader (The Late Melvin T. Walls). Again, I was young in my faith and did not understand how to war with God's Word and trust everything that He (God) had planned for me. At times, I thought God was revealing to me that the dreams I had were other people's dreams and I could not dream for myself. There was a fight going on, a tug of war in the spirit realm or in my mind. I had gifts and didn't know how to use them. Silent screams of other people's hearts put my heart in despair and dominated my thoughts. I never knew who it was. Was it a little girl needing to be heard and captured by God's unfailing love?

So, I did exactly what Pastor Powell said because, when I heard this Word before, I was not obedient and my spiritual being was not where it was supposed to be to receive the Word. Messages from the past, God's Word in the present, and my faith allowed me to see God for what He truly was, "One who never lies." Not only did my ears open but my spiritual eyes became open so that I could love the way Christ expected me to love. The bitterness was erased and the spirit of rebellion was no longer there.

I struggled for years financially because of disobedience. I struggled for years in building relationships because of pride and past hurts. I struggled because I was not disciplined enough to hear and know God's Word. The struggle for me was over.

God began to open my eyes and heart to see what He saw in me. When my eyes opened, I was able to see others the way God seen them. I was able to recognize the beauty that life brings in serving someone so wonderful. I wanted to tell the world about it.

In the summer of 2005, I was in a warfare conference at Grace Fellowship COGIC (this is after one of many revivals and a revivalist Prophetess Sun Fanin from Korea prophesied to me), shortly after on a Sunday morning, I heard a message about how when we are in trouble or when our blessings are held up in the spiritual realm God would send Michael the warring angle to fight on our behalf. Gabriel was the messenger and Michael was the warrior. The bible speaks about the angel that came to deliver his servants who trusted in God, and have changed the king's word, and yielded their bodies, that they might not serve nor worship any god, except their own God. (Daniel 3:28)

I know the pastor was really talking about Michael the angel, but I saw a vision of a young man's face on that day and later I found this handsome man to be my husband. This event happened before I had ever known him, met him or before he even asked me out on a date (through a mutual friend and sister in the Lord). No way possible did I believe that Michael was the Angel in the Bible, but God does work in mysterious ways. Sometimes I wonder why he would reveal that while my faith was being build. I thought, "Was it a joke or my imagination then?" It wasn't until late October of that year that we officially met. He didn't ask me out on a date until a month later.

In July 2006, on a warm summer evening, my husband to be picked me up from my parent's home for a date. A date without the kids for we both have children (at times we would bring our children on our dates to the parks, church, family events, restaurants, and recreation fun) but this day was different. I guess this night was very important. At the time I was unaware, the night I said yes.

We went out to dinner and then to a familiar park for a walk. He proposed to me in a gazebo in front of the pond. The most beautiful sight I'll always remember; it was better than what I even imagined it to be, my Boaz that was prophesied to me back in 1998 almost ten years later.

Life's struggles bring about trials but those trials are only to make us strong, as boys to men and girls to women are to be formed into the purpose of our creator's eyes. Prince to King, Princess to Queens, gentlemen and ladies we are formed into his image. He is so great! Our Creator knows everything. He is the Master Planner and all we are to do is trust Him and allow Him to guide us to our destiny. Was marriage the only promise to us Queens? No! There is more to life that God brings.

This book of short stories and poems is dedicated to every leader in my life. To my God and Lord and Savior Jesus Christ for never leaving me and staying by my side even when I didn't know he was there. To my husband, Michael for allowing me to be who I am as his wife and the woman God made me to be. To my daughter, Janae' (God's chosen) who is the strength of her mother's eyes, you're a ball of joy as a little girl dancing her way through life, you have become the lady that I always wanted you to be. Thank you for listening even when it didn't make sense.

To my parents, Pastor Curtis and Missionary/Evangelist Lovella Reed, for your unconditional love and support even when you didn't understand me. To my grandparents, Deacon James Reed and the late Mother Celia Mary Reed, for your love and moral teachings, guidance and instructions of family values and traditions. To all of my brothers especially Ty for fighting for me. To all of my beautiful sisters who I love so dearly you are all gifted, smart, and intelligent ladies.

To all of my nieces and nephews whom I love so dearly. To all of my aunts, uncles, cousins and friends that stood by my side in support of every dream and goal. Also, to every spiritual leader and teacher for your patience in teaching me the way of abundance. Your words of correction, instruction, guidance, wisdom, will never come unrecognized.

Most of all, to my joint family and my enemies for pushing me to a place of my true identity. The challenges were real and I know that I now have purpose. I love you all and this is to you!

IDENTITY

I will Praise Thee for I am Fearfully and Wonderfully Made

I will praise thee for I am fearfully and wonderfully made:
Marvelous are thy works;
And that my soul knoweth right well.
Psalm 139:14, KJV

Rejection is the source of everyone's insecurities, hurt, pain, and false identity of God's purpose, desire, and plan for even forming you. Before you were even thought of and in the forming of your mother's womb you had purpose. Who snatches this purpose away? The snare and the trap of your enemy the devil, It is Satan's trap for destruction. God has chosen you to complete the story of your life but, jealousy, envy, strife, hatred, mind games, generational bondages, deceit (and need I say more?) can stop His plan if you let them! You are fearfully and wonderfully made and it is up to you to know it.

Is it because of who you are? Yes! Is it because of the God you serve? Yes! Fly away, flee from, walk away, and run from these traps. Because you are who you are and only God can change others heart to love you for you, but because God's Word says it then you should believe it! Be you and embrace you with the love He placed in you his love with purpose.

YOU ARE FEARFULLY AND WONDERFULLY MADE

Marvelous are thy works…

Comparison through sibling rivalry,

Heart forming pains of hate.

Repeating of familiar substances, strong holds, and failures.

Is not this enough to tell you it's not purposed its only destruction?

Gossip, cliques, rumors, what is love?

Disconnect from those who mean you no good, they are not your God. Didn't you know that God is good and He makes no mistakes because you are fearfully and wonderfully made and marvelous are thy works; and your soul knoweth right well?

Allow God to build your confidence through His Word.

Because, He will never lead you astray,

Are you bound, broken, or confused?

It's only the hidden things that He will unfold for you.

A person of Boldness and confidence is who you are

And that's who God is forming you to be.

Hold your head up!

No longer do you have to fight, kick, holler or prove your true purpose.

He knows the plans that He has just for you.

Will you let Him lead you, guide you in to your destiny?

You are His sons and daughters and His plans are to prosper you not destroy your true purpose, your identity. For you are, I am, we all are fearfully and wonderfully made; and marvelous are thy works; and that your soul knoweth right well.

This Love IS REAL

If any man love not the Lord Jesus Christ, let him be anathema, Maranatha. 1 Cor. 16:20 (Accursed or separated from God)

He accepted me back with open arms when I left Him, and He did not destroy my name or character. He wiped away every pain of guilt and shame and did not throw me away. He told me that I was loveable, acceptable, and worth it all. This is a love hard to find. Believe me this love is real.

Nobody could understand me like He does. Nobody could treat me like he does. Nobody nowhere could love me like he does. This love is so-so-so real.

One night in my distress I was lying in my bed and his arms of comfort wrapped me in his love. He said that I was his and He was mine and told me to trust Him. As I woke out of my dream of distress I trembled in knowing that his love is real.

Real love is patient, Real love is longsuffering, Real love is forgiving; Real love heals the pain and agony of years of hurt. Real love goes into the hidden parts of the chambers of the heart and does surgery through compassion and understanding. If you haven't found this type of love yet let me tell you Girl this love is real!

He may not give me all that my heart desires but He gives me everything I need. He surprises me when I'm not toiling with fulfilling my dreams. Did I deserve it? No, but He said I was worth it!

Hey, you all I'm telling you this Love is Real!

I will never destroy a relationship so true, I will never damage a joyous connection of truth. I can never let anyone, anything, no circumstance, no heart ache, no pain, or no distress come between me and my man again because this love is Real!!!!

One of the number one things a woman cannot get rid of is man. Let me tell this man I found a love that is so, so, so, so Real.

He loves me in-spite of my shortcomings, when I have tantrums in my inpatient moments by calming me with His words of comfort to let me know His promises are real.

He surprised me one day in His glory while I was on my knees praying to Him, what a bright-bright light it was.

The comfort of knowing that He is so real,

He allowed me to see Him in His glory,

What an amazing God He is!

The creator He is. Let me tell you honey yes, this Love is Real!

My love for you dear Lord is so real. I thank you for being the patient, understanding, Master Planner of my life. Our walk together is to be everlasting. I would never leave you to hurt you. I will promise to obey your ever-lasting word that is embedded in my heart. My heart's desire is to please you and not to hurt you with fear or distrust. My Lord, my Savior, my Redeemer, let me tell you over and over again….

This Love is Real!

THE HEART OF GOD IS FULL FOR EVERYONE

This letter is to those whose heart is bruised. Sometimes we as humans do not know how to explain our pain. We kick and fight as children to explain our sorrows. Sometimes it could be years of tears shed of never being heard. Hidden thoughts saying, nobody really understands. You're reaching for love, searching for love and never receiving the type of love that you desire. The muted pains and scars of brokenness, masks of hidden emotions wanting to escape.

Prophet Isaiah said it so plain….

For the Lord thy God dwell in the high place, with him also that is of a contrite and humble spirit, to revive the heart of the contrite ones. For I will not contend for ever, neither will I be always wroth; for the spirit should fail before me, and the souls which I have made. For the iniquity of his covetousness was I wroth, and smote him I hid me, and was wroth, and he went on forwardly in the way of his heart.

I have seen his ways, and will heal you, that desire to be healed

I will lead him also, and restore comforts unto him and to his mourners.

I created the fruit of the lips; Peace, peace to him that is far off, and him that is near, saith the Lord; I will heal you. (Isaiah 57:15, KJV)

No longer live in the fear of not knowing that your God is there. He will order your steps and guide you with his compassion, love and understanding. The hidden cries are not silent they are as aloud as a baby's thirst for her mother's milk. He is the many breasted one his love is so fulfilling his heart is for everyone….

Who runs for shelter, who shields and protects, who's humbled in knowing him to restore what is lost. No more pains from despair, no more fear of lost you have all in knowing him. He's all the Love you need. His heart is large!

The heart of God is full for everyone!

May your soul RIP Mrs. Carolyn Jackie Reed. Message from Father Gary

OUR TRUST IS IN YOU

When it seems as if our world is upside down and our struggles have been too hard to bear

Our Trust Is In You

When our enemies are out for revenge to fulfill their vindictive plans of the unaware.

To kill, steal, and destroy and should I tell you the floods of their own guilt and sorrows?

Our Trust Is In You

When our back is pushed to the wall and when there is no more kick left or room to escape

Our Trust Is In You

The pointing of fingers not knowing their own destructions

Our Trust Is In You

When our identity is lost for other's wealth and power, snatched for their social gain

Our Trust Is In You

Destroyed through mind games and life's gain and pride

Our Trust Is In You

When all hope is gone and there is no light we look to you because we know it was not you to destroy our sight

We know with all of our heart and mind that

Our Trust Is In You!

It took me the longest to trust something that I could not see, feel or touch. God's amazing love taught me to put my trust in him. With my whole heart, I began to seek after him in return he gave me the very desires of my heart.

It is only normal to trust your leaders, parents, church, government, friends, and people in law. But, to put your trust in God he will unfold the mysteries and hidden truth you've always looked for. There's never confusion there.

My heart was like stone and I couldn't trust anyone. I internalized everything and formed a norm in my mind to be able to function. This only caused me to be oppressed and depressed. I didn't like people and people didn't like me. It was hard to form relationships. I became an introvert.

Crying inside and speaking my heart, which was bitter and broken. Whispers of loud chaos of gossip heard. This hurt me the most. Never let the right hand know what the left hand is doing. Who are you to trust when this happens? God, he will never leave you or forsake you.

He is not the author of confusion Satan is. He only comes in to kill still and destroy; and believe me, when he does this, he has succeeded his plans. But God always will form an escape for you if you trust him, like I did. I had to say enough is enough!

I then heard a voice saying, "Will you trust me? At the time, I thought it was my mind playing tricks on me. I heard the question again but this time it was louder asking me, "Monique will you trust me?" I then replied, "God I trust you." Many of nights I cried, "Lord you have to fix it for me."

This is what I prayed over and over again. I said, to him Lord, "I'll get out of the way and ask you to have your way with my heart, and my mind. Fix it! I trust you with my whole heart, with my whole mind, and with all my might. When my strength is weakened make me strong. I trust you Lord."

The Lord your God loves you that much. Listen to the words of His heart, it's all written in His Word. His words do not lie; only people do because they have fallen in to the traps of Satan's deceit for destruction.

God builds up. He never tears down! Always remember to trust in the Lord your God.

MEET ME BEHIND THE VEIL

Meet me Behind the Veil

No demons will be magnified there.

In his presence, there's a radiance of glory.

No man's glory but God's glory will be there.

There's joy there and peace there, behind the veil…

Just like Moses, you can communicate with the Father,

Behind the Veil

No more fading away because of sins of evil communication, jealousy, envy, and strife.

Will you go with me?

There's no idol worship there, only God's presence and His bright radiance of light.

Meet me behind the Veil

The weights and oh yes, every burden is lifted there!

He will wipe away the pride of life that magnified Satan's plans for destruction

And in his presence, there's no overindulgence or greed there.

Come go with me behind the Veil

He will take away un-forgiveness, guilt, shame, and defeat. Every dark cloud will be brought down below your feet.

A perfect stillness so you can hear the words that will bring laughter and revive every heartbeat.

Will you go with me? Will you trust me to show you that, He is true?

Come go with me behind the Veil

He will unravel the hidden truth with his word

He will show you the hidden things that will enlighten and bless you.

Come go with me behind the veil

What a wonderful place it is to rest in his presence, to trust our heavenly Father

No more tears of pain only tear of joy, there's even healing there.

Come and go and bow down with me before the father behind the veil,

He said that He will take you there. Will you go with me behind the veil? Come and go with me behind the veil….

In my singleness before marriage I listened to a great evangelist who led me to worship, Prophetess Juanita Bynum, singing Behind the Veil. This song ministered to me when I was confused in my sins, very young in my salvation walk, and not knowing where to run. I went to a church service, and after church, I stayed on the altar, prayed, fasted before God, and repented over and over again. Every religious act that I did, to receive God as my father. I really didn't know how to rest.

I believe I did it out of fear. The Bible told me to fear God and I did but, because I was so broken- hearted I could not hear him. Was it pride? It was the very spirit of stubbornness, and rebellion that closed my ears. It was the spirit of depression that oppressed me to no limits.

I would read His Word and could not line it up according to my life because of un-forgiveness. No one really understood my pain. I was in a whirl wind, twirling with every spirit of darkness, not knowing how to get out or through the storm. I found myself in traps of failure and didn't know how to see God for what he was, my savior and redeemer through Jesus Christ.

When I found out that I was one of the remnants who He was calling forth and heard His voice I became aware of who He was in my life. He was no longer in the box of what I made him to be. He was the Holy Spirit that I needed and what I sought after.

Many of nights I found myself at the Watch of the Lord Service to just be in His presence and to quiet out the demons entrapped in my mind. I stayed there overnight crying out and praying and sometimes even sleeping. But, God saw my faithfulness and granted me my heart desires, Healing for the sorrow and pain. There were so many provisions made. Bills were paid,

I was able to provide for my family, prayers were answered, and I was finally able to trust him.

He met me there in his atonement behind the vail. What a wonderful place to be still before God in the radiance of his love and peace. No longer was I tormented. No longer did I listen to the destruction of men/women's words that stirred my heart to not receive from the Father. No longer did I accept the laughter and teasing of others. Because I was in God's glory realm, I went past the clouds. I saw the sparkling diamonds in the air. I felt the tingling filling throughout my body. I finally knew He was real.

From that day forth I've been telling others of my experience with God the Father. What a wonderful and marvelous place to be when everything around you seem to be twirling you around and upside down. He will place you on the path of righteousness where you belong in his peace! In His, glory behind the veil.

CHAMPION OF FAITH

Now faith is!

I have the faith to!

Without faith, it is in impossible to please God.

Abraham, Isaac, Sarah, Enoch, Mary, Joseph, Paul all exemplify this type of champion I describe.

If I had the faith to move mountains.

What great faith! Exclaimed a blind man's desire to see fulfilled…

The impossible inventions would describe this type of champion….

Faith? What is it? When you cannot see, believe or achieve the things that your mother or father dream. What about your own?

When the valleys are so low and dark you can hardly see light. You still seem to walk in peace. Is this the type?

Hearing echoes of cries of the repeated pain of someone else's lies.

Time after time deserted screams yet the only thing is to hold on to is his promises especially when left alone to unscramble the clues of another person's storms.

Is it this type of champion I describe?

Champions of faith are those who find a way to climb every mountain that comes their way.

They run through the valleys because they are never comfortable there.

They pray through a storm because they believe it will pass.

They plan for the end because it's promised to come to pass.

They believe in a word or a song.

Champions of faith tells others how to reach each goal because of their own.

Champions of faith are warriors, dreamers, endure-rs, they are true to themselves and everyone else!

Now faith is a champion of things hope for and the evidence of a champion stories to tell to help other champions grow their own.

Champions of faith tell your story, testify, tell your accomplishments, you are an overcomer!

Show your strengths!

Never say you are weak!

Because it's a lie a champion never quit, just fly!

Know you are a Champion from birth who ever tells you differently they are a lie!

Champion of faith, you know who you are.

Achieve grow and show who you describe.

A champion of faith that's all!

Your rewards are great, and others will know that your trust is in God.

So, Go! Go!

Champion tell your story of healings, deliverances, miracles, and should I say more?

You are the champion of faith grow!

Champion of faith you are!

BROKEN BUT NOT TORN APART

Broken but not torn into

millions of pieces scattered abroad…

Broken dreams, broken desires, and plans for a future that was started from a tot

Scattered like shells of an egg not knowing where to start putting them back together again…

Broken but not torn apart

Puzzles of my heart divided in trillions of pieces of hidden emotions driven by battered pains and scars

Hidden from years of covered facades

Masks of many people because of rejection

Broken but not torn apart

Whoever knew the great counselor to mend my broken-ness

It was never glued to fall apart again or stitched by threads of man- made methods to make me whole again

It takes his word of encouragement to mend all brokenness

Could it be he that shatters all dreams? No!

To make you lose all identity of wholeness? No!

Never again will one be broken

Never again will one be torn

When He promised wholeness to all who believe

Every broken experience made me to be the solid and the whole person I am today

Yes, I was broken but never torn apart

What does God say to those whose spirit is broken and has a broken contrite heart?

He will heal the broken in heart and bind-eth up again

He spoke through Isaiah the prophet and said that he has come to bind up the broken-hearted,

To proclaim liberty to the captives…

So, what do I say to the broken heart? Run to the Rock for there is a sure foundation there!

He will never break your heart!

He will free you from any brokenness

He will save you from all destruction

He will keep you whole and safe in his arms

Free from all hate and confusion

Once broken but whole again

YOU ARE AN OVERCOMER FROM BIRTH

Him that overcometh will I make a pillar in the temple of my God, and he shall go no more out: and I will write upon him the name of my God, and the name of the city of my God, which is new Jerusalem, which cometh down out of heaven from my God: and I will write upon him my new name.
Revelation 3:12

What is an overcomer?

Are you that woman or man who strives above every challenge to reach his or her goal through life's struggles?

Do not give up and throw in the towel when the pain is so strong and echoes of defeat tries to hold you down? When trial and tribulations come to make you strong and equip you for God's promise? God is showing you your birth right, throughout the storm. You are an overcomer from birth!

Do you know your birth right overcomer? Who stole the vision of promises? Have you told someone lately that you are an overcomer?

Before God formed you in the belly of your mother's womb, you were an overcomer! Do you hear your mother's words that structured your purpose? It's in the meaning of your name.

Jesus Christ has made you an overcomer!

An overcomer is one who runs to the end when the race seems like it's over. He or she strives to the top when they are at the very bottom. They are the ones who have been told no and God said yes. They are the last that became first because of their obedience to God's Word.

You are an overcomer from birth.

When the going gets rough and it seems like there's no more tears and God whispers to you keep going because you're almost there. An overcomer listens to His Word, and knows that it was God giving them strength to endure and pass every given test.

An overcomer shows their strength like an eagle and with their faith they fly above the rest. They are seekers, they are watchers, they are worshipers, they show forth the praise of Him who brought them out of darkness into His marvelous light, and they are the pillars that keep one from falling.

They are achievers, they are dreamers, and they are lovers of God's word. They are the latter and former rain; they are the remnant that is blessed by God.

They are humble giants; they are never too proud; they are overcomers from birth.

You are, I am, we are all Overcomer's from birth.

Inspired by Pastor W. S. Foster, III from a message preached in 2013 "You are An Overcomer."

MY ATTITUDE IS MY ALTITUDE

Your attitude should be the same as that of Christ Jesus: Who, being in very nature God, did not consider equality with God something to be grasped, but made himself nothing, taking the very nature of a servant, being made in human likeness. And being found in appearance as a man, he humbled himself and became obedient to death-- even death on a cross! Therefore, God exalted him to the highest place and gave him the name that is above every name, that at the name of Jesus every knee should bow, in heaven and on earth and under the earth, and every tongue confess that Jesus Christ is Lord, to the glory of God the Father. –Philippians 2:5-11 (NIV)

Today I was reminded of a little girl who really didn't have as much as others. She always saw others with the finest, the nicest, the good, and the best things that some may call life treasures. She gave her all but never really could see the benefits of her giving, due to competition and comparison that she heard in the loud chaos of others. Was she blinded by pride?

Very often she would envy others and became very sadden by what God uncovered. Her heart became sore and hardened, and many of times she found herself questioning God, "How can they benefit and receive when they are constantly moaning, grumbling, complaining, and controlling?" "Who is really in control?" Doubt kicked in. Hatred kicked in. Defeat tried to have his course over the mind-boggling scenarios from life circumstances that caused spiritual blindness.

One day, she became very tired of fighting against the grains that had her choking and grasping for air. She was tired of trying to cut corners to achieve. She wanted to strive for the best. She became humbled through repentance and as she went, she was healed of every wound of brokenness and bitterness. Her ears became opened and God wiped away the cobwebs that had her blinded. She didn't know she was in such a world of darkness. Still, she really couldn't trust but really wanted to receive everything that God had for her. Someone told her that it would only come through obedience. It was very hard for her to trust this person, she thought to herself, "Trust who you and why?"

God questioned her one day saying, "Do you trust me?" At first, she couldn't recognize the voice because of Satan's camouflage and mockery. Can I say the demons had to flee!!! She responded by saying, "Yes, I will trust you but, God I am so angry!"

The tears fell and the pain increased, the attitude became worse. Yet, she continued to be obedient to only an extent. She couldn't let go of her enemies. She wanted them to pay for the crime of her pain. They were murderers, thieves, and their crime was always hidden. "How can they get away with this?" She asked God. God, said, "Was it my grace that set you free? But, they know right from wrong? Who is the author of confusion? Are they as human as you?" God opened her eyes from the prejudice that had her bound. He told her Vengeance is mine says the Lord of Hosts. I will fight for you. Just praise me throughout your test. You will come out victorious!"

This is when she realized she had to release it all to God saying, "God you have to take this pain away. My heart is like a rock, although, I said I knew you and heard your voice, this pain is unbearable." God said, "There's much work to do my daughter. Didn't you say you were a servant for me? Do you see the vineyard? Don't you hear the cries of the innocent just as you were?" The tears came falling down her face. She finally, heard God's voice from years of fasting, praying, and toiling. It was no longer an act of faith. Faith began to work. The character and fruit began to operate through his love. The meaning of true discipleship became very clear through wisdom and knowledge of His Word, *"If anyone loves him, he will keep his word; and his Father will love them, and with Christ you will come to him and make your abode with him." (John 14:23, KJV)* She could do things she could never imagine doing. Your attitude is your altitude for success!

Your attitude, (A settled way of thinking or feeling about someone or something, typically one that is reflected in a person's behavior), is your altitude (The height of an object or point in relation to sea level or ground level), for success (The accomplishment of an aim or purpose). It's something that you really cannot hide especially if it's a bad one. It's something that cannot be covered with phony smiles. God always has a way to show and tell the truth and reveal the darkness of someone else's sins and erase combativeness. No longer did this young lady have to play the role of someone else's story. The charades of hate, evil, and despair was erased. She came into the knowledge of how to achieve success. It was with a good attitude. Your attitude is your altitude for success!

Your attitude should reflect the character of Christ. When driven to your worse through others from the remembrance of pain and childhood spats, your character should be controlled with Christ's compassionate heart of love. What does one do when one cannot hear the heart or read between the lines? They should press beyond how they feel and know that there's no pain that God cannot heal and know that all things work together for the good to those who believe. Then, too forgive yourself and others for their ignorance of the God you serve.

What if one doesn't believe? Just like the young lady in this story...never doubt God and know that He will hear your cry, see your tears, and know your pain. He will bring you out. Always look at the good. Never focus on the bad or the past and know that if you ask, seek, knock, He will answer. You will find and the doors will be opened unto you in Jesus' name. Always keep a good attitude and you can climb to the top.

Won't God, do it? Yes, He will. Because I believe God.... Jesus is our example. Stay humble before God, consider yourself as nothing when it comes to him, and be exalted with him. The elevation comes from above. No one really knows how God does it all. You must step out of the way and allow him to do the work. Just like this young lady did. She could do things that she would never imagine. Know that your attitude is your altitude for your success!

Inspired by a message from Pastor W. S. Foster, III

Mend What is Broken, "Lord Take This Heart of Mine and Fix It."

I ran to the altar

I stayed on the altar

I prayed there crying out to the Lord take this heart of mine and fix it!

I stood naked before you meaning, that there was nothing I could ever cover

I cried to you

The Wonderful Counselor you are

You showed me your love and concern

You held my hand to let me know that you were there

My father, my daddy, my best friend

The things you helped me to understand was unimaginable

You showed me that I was worth drying every tear

This was almost mind boggling to know you were so near

You allowed me to know that your love was irreplaceable

In the day when I cried you answered me, and strengthened my soul

Just like David the King, I was your princess and was well worth it

You mended what was broken and you did the surgery no one else could do

If I can scream on the mountain top leading others to you, telling them to...

Cry aloud lift up your heart unto the Lord tell Him your deepest secrets

Open your ears to his words and know that He is God; you will never go wrong there

When the temper comes, run to the altar He will dry up every one of your tears

Tell him about all of your troubles He is there

Cry aloud Lord take this heart of mine and fix it!

He will remove all stones, and push out all blocks where his love and compassion can flow free again!

He has mended what is broken and fixed my heart again!

Mend what is broken Lord Take their hearts and fix it?

SOLDIER YOU ARE

I'm a soldier in the army of the Lord…I'm a soldier in the army of the Lord…I'm a soldier in his army. If I die let me die in the army. I got my war clothes on in the army of the Lord….

(1980 Group Together)

What is a Soldier? Is it one who goes through the battles and war for his or her country?

Heeding and following through to every command their officer is giving?

One who goes into battle and knows who their enemy is, warring until he's down and

Striving for victory?

One who is equipped for battle, with the breastplate of righteousness, garment of praise, helmet of salvation, suited up with every metal?

One who is focused on the field and armed to attack the enemy with the sword, God's Holy Word.

Who needs a gun in this fight? When the power of God's hand is upon you guiding you through this battle, just follow his commands.

You are a soldier when you protect your camp,

The others who are on solid ground in the field of faith standing on God's promises

Who needs a grenade when the anointing destroys all yokes?

Soldier you are

Fighting and standing when the enemy is encamped all around you,

shooting you with darts and fire of hate

When all that is left to do is speak a word and his warring angels are released to defend you.

Don't you know he will fight this battle for you? Marching through the fields chanting songs that will send your enemy back to his camp!

Soldier you are

When you are able to go in power to snatch back everything he has stolen.

Soldier you are

As you were

Go forth, be brave, be strong, hold on, because you are victorious!

Soldier fight the good fight of faith!

You win in every fight because you are in the Lord's Army.

Soldier you are!

My Best Friend

Who is a best friend to a man?

Is it someone you hang out with daily to shoot the breeze and talk about the ladies?

Who is a best friend to a woman?

Is it someone you trust and have confident in? The one who knows the innermost secrets you share with?

I really couldn't tell you that a best friend is one you cherish or love, especially when friendship is dependent upon a man, woman, your favorite toy or animal.

The days, the months, the years, and decades between the times one shares.

The laughter, the tears, and the time

Can I say you were not there?

No not at all!

The tough times through the years of distress

The heartaches the pain and each and every cry for help were you there?

My best friend for years was dependent on the comfort of knowing you were there.

When I'm afraid, alone, in my quiet times, and warring times you were there my friend.

Who is a best friend?

Is it I?

Is it you?

Is it my mom?

Is it my dad?

Is it my dog?

Is it my husband?

Is it my wife?

Is it who?

My best friend, thank you for never leaving me alone and teaching me the importance of loyalty and trust.

MAN!!!

Called to God's purpose to lead and to guide with wisdom and knowledge, show us your authority through love and wisdom from above.

Is it the strength in your arms that we desire? Is it the figure shaped in the temple of the unknown?

Show us who lies behind your eyes. Speak to us the words that form our heart to trust yours?

Man, with great stature.

Man, with great power that we all desire.

Man, with great wisdom from above.

Man, with a covering from Heaven who knows how to cover his love.

Man is what we desire with God's great power; a gifted man with confidence, knowledge, love, compassion, and understanding of what women, ladies, and girls' desire.

Come forth Man of God Come Forth!

A wise man will hear and will increase learning; and a man of understanding shall attain unto wise counsels. -Proverbs 1:5

IF I WERE YOUR QUEEN

If I were your Queen and you were my King I would feel the love when you wrap me in your arms with your strength of love.

If I were your queen and you were my King I would hear your sweet words that whisper in my ears to let me know you love me.

The whispers that will let anyone's heart move to dancing

Wrap me in your arms my King,

Twirl me in the wind and let me hear the beats of your love again

My King!

I was thinking about the comfort that the God of Comfort gives. The sweetness he brings, and the joy one experiences in knowing him through Jesus Christ. He's the best and wonderful friend one could ever have. He is the savior of many who believe in him and the Great Messiah. There's nobody on earth like him.

I was also thinking about the relationships in marriage, he allows us to have in knowing him. I was in a quiet place and felt all alone. I wasn't really alone I just felt alone. I knew then that they were always there. The two men of my life God the Father and my husband. He wanted me to imagine being their Queen because I am and I know that. Just like the fairy tale of my dreams. We all have fairy tales/dreams that come true, we just have to learn how to make dreams happen.

I am a romantic by nature and no one should ever come in between a woman's love between husband and wife. We as women should never become too busy or distracted to not recognize our human rights and spiritual rights. It's who we are. No one should ever come in to tell us anything different or snatch it away.

God knows the desires of our hearts and he does all things well. The Bible speaks about the Obedience in love. It says we gain confidence towards God. "And whatsoever we ask, we receive of him, because we keep his commandments, and do those things that are pleasing in his sight." (I John 3: 22)

I don't know about you but I'd rather receive in meekness through obedience. There's greater rewards and you don't never have to manipulate in order to receive God's promises. He always knows how to make us happy and feel like the Princess and the Queen that we are.

Can you imagine the King twirling you around speaking sweet words of encouragement that only beautifies you? I can! He will if only you let down your guards and trust in him. Just Imagine!

OWE NO ONE AN APOLOGY FOR WHO GOD HAS CREATED YOU TO BE

Shame:

Noun: A feeling of guilt, regret, or sadness that you have because you know you have done something wrong. The ability to feel guilt, regret, or embarrassment. Shame is feeling dishonor or disgrace.

Verb: To cause (someone) to feel ashamed. To force (someone) to act in a specified way by causing feelings of shame or guilt. (Merriam-Webster)

Owe No One An Apology for Who God has Created You To Be!

I apologize that you cannot see my beauty, my talent, the little girl, the little boy, the lady, the young man, the woman, the man that God has created me to be.

I apologize that my hair is not like yours, the color of my eyes is not like yours, or my skin is not the color of the likeness you have structured your eyes to see.

I apologize that you cannot see the knowledge, intellect, or wisdom of God's Beauty.

Yet, there is no apology when others cannot see with the love of God's eyes because of their own hidden scars and pride.

Owe no one an apology of who God has created you to be. We are all formed and created in the image of his identity if you believe.

So, owe no man or woman an apology for whom God has created you to be.

Can you see…

Your own beauty?

No longer hide it because you are qualified to glorify your creator who shines through you.

Owe no one, no man, no woman an apology for God has created you and is forming you to the likeness of who He has created you to be!

When God revealed to me who I was broken and who I was whole I began going around apologizing to everyone. Then He opened my eyes to other people's insecurities. It's easier to point out others flaws and not identify your own. I mean people were in high royal places having their own demons they battled with. The one big one was insecurities through low self-esteem.

I was humbled enough to recognize my own and not point out others. I then became an introvert and internalized my thoughts and they became sores. I could never speak my mind and when I did it was like scissors cutting on everyone else's character and sometimes my own.

Because I was surrounded by my judgers who I entrusted to be my friends I started to speak like they spoke, think how they thought, and see what they saw. My enemies were within and I had to break away and embrace me again. Boy was this tough especially, when I didn't know where to begin.

One day I was hearing this enemy. I began to speak the heart of them. I hated myself and knew that it was not I. They (my enemies) wanted me dead and not alive. So, I disconnected myself from my worst; judgers, critics, haters, doubters, vain glory people who never saw the beauty in anyone else but themselves, my enemies.

(II Timothy 3:1-9 This know also, that in the last day's perilous times shall come. For men shall be lovers of their own selves, covetous, boasters, proud, blasphemers, disobedient to parents, unthankful, unholy, without natural affection, trucebreakers, false accusers, incontinent, fierce, despisers of those that are good, Traitors, heady, high minded, lovers of pleasures more than lovers of God; Having a form of godliness, but denying the power thereof: from such turn, away. For of this sort are they which creep into houses, and lead captive silly women laden with sins, led away with divers lusts, Ever learning, and never able to come to the knowledge of the truth. Now as Jannes and Jambres withstood Moses, so do these also resist the truth: men of corrupt minds, reprobate concerning the faith. But

they shall proceed no further: for their folly shall be manifest unto all men, as theirs also was.)

Unknowingly, I began to talk like them, look like them, and was very lost. Where did I go? Was I in a place of idol worship? Was it wicked to show the reflections of them? Did I belong? Do I have any identity? What about my beliefs? Who was forming me like this? Was it my own pride or theirs?

I heard myself and the words. I said, these are not my words I don't think of myself this way. The God I served, my counselor JESUS met me in the tub one day and I began to pray and ask him to change my words and thoughts. I ask him to help me see me as he saw me.

I began to cry and said, "I love me!" I looked at myself from the reflection of the faucet. A not so perfect person in many people's eyes but the perfect person God made me to be. I began to hug myself and to kiss me. I kissed my arms and my legs. That deceitful devil wanted me to die, but I wanted to give him a black eye. I wanted to prove to him that the greater one that was in me is Greater than he that is in the whole world. (I John 4:4) Satan is a defeated foe!

No longer did I have to turn from the reflection of who I saw in that mirror again. God's grace perfects us. He gives us time to improve our imperfections. He also allows us to love his own creations you and me. I love to be beautified by the Holy Spirit because that's when true beauty shines. We are the reflection of our Maker. Won't you allow him to shine?

God's Eyes

God's eye is watching over us as we speak. He sees everything! This makes me wonder what He thinks. Do I bring tears to His eyes when I forget that He is watching? Is He getting angry and jealous when He is not glorified? What about God's eyes?

God's eyes hold the mystery of the unknown. He will not reveal to kill, still or destroy. God's eyes are very compassionate, empathetic, and loving. No one has really seen them but He reveals himself through others, the sky, and even you if you believe.

God's eyes will tell you no lie. He speaks the truth and never hides. They sparkle so bright and reveal the love that only He gives.

God's eyes are never confusing they lead, guide, and direct you; along the path of righteousness, happiness, and never darkness.

God's eyes are as clear as the blue sky. One can see what He sees and the brightness He only brings. Don't you see the shining stars that He reflects? It's light and bright. It's like Him winking at us.

God's eyes draw you in and never are deceiving to hypnotize you to do wrong or evil. They are beautiful, they do beautiful things, and they show you His beauty.

God's eyes always correct in love and sometimes in anger. So, always look for them to be happy and bring Him honor. They are never like man's eyes they are God's eyes!

Many Faces Of Me

Who defines me? What defines me? Can I see myself hidden behind the many faces of me? The social butterfly that lights up the room and turns many faces and who hears echoes of torment through fear, because I just want to be me.

A face that hides to allow others to shine to receive their own identity could that be me?

The career person who climbs above economic burdens and political machines in order to provide for their family could that be me?

Reaching out to others no matter of their human identity to help and to show the love that hides behind this beauty can that be me?

We put on faces to fit in, to blend in a big crowd, to get through the hatred crimes of bitterness that holds us down, bound and afflicted of Satan's plans for destruction of failure that cannot be me!

Many faces of skin colors; white, yellow, light brown, dark brown, red…

Who tries to tell their identity? Don't they know? Can't they see?

To be held back so others can stride forward because of their social significance and acceptance in who's eyes?

Facades that hold back the tears and fears with forced smiles and brokenness

Faces of shame because of the chaos of the powers of the unknown

Is it because of a name? Oh, can I tell you about the stigmas that were formed before birth to structure my heart to make me who I am…

The face to describe is His transformation through the Holy-Ghost power to make a person into their identity of humility or humbleness is that me?

A mother struggling for work to overcome a classification to hold her below the normal ties, and formal ties, of a society that works

Many faces of…

Holding back years of rejection trying to find acceptance and not knowing who to turn to during a time of mental oppression,

Disguised among many not knowing her identity wanting so much that life had to offer. Not knowing how to talk what is the right verbal communication were all odds against me?

Running, striving, overcoming every trap of Satan's entrapments, many camps of hostages, warring against a struggle of darkness, which was captured by a savior, given another chance to prove my place in society

Overcoming an identity of a slave mindset and poverty, trusted by a love that no one can recognize because of their own need to strive

Climbing mountains, crossing the dry desert, swimming and treading above waters so that I can accomplish every promised plan, are the many faces of me.

The lawyer

The doctor

The business women

The servant

The Woman of God

The Man of God

The child looking for a leader

The mother

The father

The entrepreneur

The leader

Many faces that cannot hide the strength that lies within

to overcome every struggle that shines His power not ours! It's me can you see?

The many faces of me!

PRAISE IS YOUR WEAPON

God despises a man or woman who doubts him. When He has given you the keys of faith, and you as his chosen does not use it.

If Jesus can turn water into wine and give you power to move mountains and you still won't praise God.

Is it anyone else's fault that these elements have not been used?

Why can't you see past the black and white? Can't you see the colors in the air?

Who has stolen your focus; is it pride and greed?

I hear music, can't you?

Why can't you think outside of the box?

Faith is the substance of things hoped for and the evidence of things unseen

Who has blinded you man, woman, or you?

Who told you, you couldn't strive high and reach the sky?

Did they belong in your present, now, or future anyway?

Can you get them out of your circle? You are a joint heir unto God through Jesus Christ not your enemies?

Are you your worst enemy or your own friend?

Who has connected you to so much hurt?

Who's contradicting God's word when it comes to your life?

Can I tell you they don't belong, never did, never will?

Critics be gone in Jesus's name or keep coming with your lies it's only paving my way for success and making your own destruction

Judge not for you will be judged

Hours on your knees praying and never seeing any results

When you rise words of doubt, hate, and defeat have deafened the ears of your God

Contemplating, toiling, emotional outbursts

Can you hear yourself?

If God said it, that settles it

Who's leading, who's on first, the ball is in your corner and the bases are full Lead us all home…

He's calling you forth man, woman, leader…

He's bringing you out

Do you have praise on your lips?

Can I hear you shout, Hallelujah, thank you Jesus for your deliverance?

He wants to elevate you and promote you to places in Him where you have never been

Who has their dancing shoes on?

I'm ready, are you?

Can you hear me now?

Let's go!

He's pulling at your heart; can you feel him?

Do you hear His words?

I do, He's saying

Come forth

Come forth Man of God, Woman of God

I have been calling you into a place where you've never been

I am elevating you and equipping you just follow I'll lead you trust me and go

I have given you the keys

Praise is your weapon!

You Can Never Come In Between a Girl and Her Music Come on Let's Dance!

Let the drum roll begin let the music play come on let's dance!

I feel free when I can move to the beat of the bass drum and snare, the loud cymbals that start my feet to moving.

Can you hear the trumpet aloud?

What about that bass guitar that sounds like the beat of a heart and brings life in every sound?

The high pitch of a piccolo or the jazziness of a saxophone

I hear music in the air.

Words from songs that lift my spirits

You can never come between a girl and her Music

Who wants to dance? Come on let's shake it off, stump it out, and leap for joy!

When I'm in my quiet time I can hear the music

When I am a sleep it wakes me up

When I want to celebrate

Come on let's jam!

Can you fill it in the air?

It drives every emotion to happiness and freedom Don't you try to hold me down and stop my freedom!

A girl's choice of music brings laughter, it begins the bobbing of the head, it gives peace, and she can get lost in every twirl and turn.

Do you want to fly with me?

Come on let's dance!

Believe me you will never come between a girl and her music, let's dance!

BITTER, BATTERED, BLACK AND WOUNDED

But he will say I am not a prophet; I am a tiller of the ground, for a man sold me as a slave in my youth. And one will say to him what are these wounds between your arms? Then he will say Those with which I was wounded In the house of my friends. -Zachariah 13:6, KJV

Ladies, keep your name keep your identity and self-worth. Know your beauty and the person that lies within the heart and mind. It should be your maker, God the Father through Jesus Christ.

A bitter, battered, black woman who was wounded let down her guard one day. This young lady was naïve and thought everyone could be trusted. She put her life in the hands of others and not in the hands of her creator.

Because of the hurt, she experienced a great deal of un forgiveness. The pain rooted in her heart. Years of running, never knowing where to find shelter, she became bitter.

Years of trusting others to pave her destiny falling into the enemy's hands because of cycles of the unknown. Fighting her way through, trying to find love and ended up battered.

Wounds, heaviness, and shackles never healed, lightened, or broken.

One kept saying she's cursed.

Others never knew their own pain

Burdens taken from others unknowingly structured a life of a beautiful black woman.

She never knew her own beauty she hid the tears and pain

Forced into a lifestyle of other people demons.

Whose words, were they? Can you hear them?

Acting out emotions that structured a person of the unknown

A bitter, battered, black woman

Found her way to the altar tried to leave her burdens with the Lord but, was uncovered for other people self-righteousness.

She became even bitter because no one really knew how to peel away each layer that was formed.

One day she came into contact with the Man of God his name is Wonderful Counselor, her redeemer.

He began to unravel the truth through her trust in His Word and spirit.

He told her to let go all of her pain, but she replied they were my friends and He told her he was her friend.

He asked her Will you trust me? Though they slay you, will you still trust me?" Each time that bitter, black, wounded woman let down her guard the attacks came even harder because the truth had to be covered.

Who is the truth? Jesus Christ!!

It took years and little baby steps by faith had to kick in.

Jesus came to her again and said, "Lady, Woman of God, can you hear me?

Will you trust me now?"

This was after blessings and favor had come her way. Yet, the mistrust stayed because of the scars from others welted on her back. Was this doubt?

Wounds unhealed, heaviness that caused stiffness in the body, the life of Christ that tried to squeeze the breath out of her.

Woman of God, your healing and miracle is right at the door. No longer do you have to hide the God in you. No longer do you have to fight a defeated battle. The battle is not yours, it is the Lord's. Let it go!

He asked her again. "Lady will you trust me? I know your fears and I even see your tears." Let go and let God have his way.

Trust in the Lord! He paid the price so that you do not have to suffer any longer.

Betrayal came to him and He took the pain for you.

Be wise; submit under his authority, let down your guard only to Jesus Christ.

That young lady laid at the feet of her savior one day at the altar. He in his glory took the pain away as he promised. He paved a way for her life. He even gave the innocence of her youth back. He said it was because of her sacrificial prayers, dedication, and loyalty that granted her freedom again.

Lady, Woman of God, Prophetess, never let your guard down to the wounded. Protect your heart with the breast plate of righteousness. Know that you are loved and watch the love of your life give you the very desires of your heart.

He is the King that you never had. He will redeem you from the years that the locust warm, caterpillar, and palmer worm have eaten away.

Meaning, He will grant you the life that had true purpose from birth.

Once wounded, once battered, once broken, and still Black, bold, and beautiful through Jesus Christ!

HAND ME ANOTHER BRICK

Inspired by Dr. Charles R. Swindoll book, "Hand Me Another Brick Timeless Lessons on Leadership, How Effective Leaders Motivate Themselves and Others.

Hand me another Brick and let's together build a wall to keep sin out. A world that's full of love and compassion and empathy for others. That's what it is all about.

Together building more and greater leaders in our society who are not destroyed by the pride and arrogance that brings self-infliction, psychological distress, sin through gossip and hate. Hand me another brick to help build a wall to keep my enemies out.

A wall that will bring good solid foundation through the Word and truth that does not compromise and contradict God's Word. Building true men and women who know the power of prayer and what God can do, who live to worship. Praying prayers that does not have racism, prejudices, or manipulate God. Thinking of not of only themselves but others too, fulfilling the promises of God.

Hand me another brick to build up children who do not fear evil but trust God and leading others to that altar, who are not influenced by idolatry and falling into the traps of Satan's plans for destruction!

Hand me another brick to keep hate out of the minds and hearts of the innocent, by not gossiping and forming them to be bitter. Hand me another brick to keep sin and mine and your enemy out, so that sound minds can go forth in true worship.

Hand me another brick to build up the house of God for true worship that will only glorify God through Jesus Christ our redeemer, savior, healer, and provider. Hand me another brick to build up the broken hearted, the destructed mindset, and the ones who never even thought they had a purpose for living.

How many of you have a brick to start building the New Wall for Jerusalem? I am that leader that God has called out to lead others no matter what opposition, no matter what distraction that tried to stop me, no matter what chaos I heard that was through gossip, and overcoming my enemies trap for destruction. I know I have been built for a purpose to lead.

Here's a brick let's build together.

I Want To Be More Than Just A Trophy On Your Side!

I want to be more than just a trophy on your side.

Your midnight swing

Didn't you know that I am a good thing

Can't you see?

If you don't let me go so I can show someone else

me!

I will show you of my worth

I'm living my dream

I'm living my purpose

Too much time has been wasted.

Didn't you know that I am a Queen and my daddy is a King?

I am of royalty

False hopes

Fake dreams

Ambitions of some other woman's dream or can I say spirit

Hello, do you know me yet?

This is not a dating game

I can't be your bachelorette

In tears crumbled

Broken and in disgust ever again!

Loose me or win me

Who is the game?

I'm sorry, what's the name of this game?

Man, I know my worth!

Is it that I make you look good?

Is it all about your manly hood?

Man, I know my worth!

Just because you didn't see it or dare to recognize it

I am a diamond in disguise.

I do in all many ways

Most of all I do love me more

I know my worth.

It's sad to say you never did

Good bye or man up!

I am more than a trophy on your side!

A Humble Heart Will Always……

"Do nothing from rivalry or conceit, but in humility count others more significant than yourselves. Let each of you look not only to his own interests, but also to the interests of others. Have this mind among yourselves, which is yours in Christ Jesus, who, though he was in the form of God, did not count equality with God a thing to be grasped, but made himself nothing, taking the form of a servant, being born in the likeness of men. ..." Philippians 2:3-11, ESV

The Bible also says, that they who humble themselves will be exalted. (1 Peter 5:6). So many times, people want to over talk, prove their positions, and reprove by trying to be the center of attention. They are not humble. They are the loud ones. The ones who usually purposely stand out in a crowd. They are ones of conceit.

A humble heart will always be exalted. A humble mind will always be heard. God always has an ear for those who comes before Him in humility. There's never hidden truth for He knows all and hears all.

The problem with conceit is that there's so much focus on self. One would build their minds and compare with others due to their own insecurities. We all fall in this trap at times because of pride. Is it right? Who knows if anyone really recognizes it to being an abnormal behavior.

One would say snatch out the heart and put it on the back burner. There is no time to feel in your inner emotions. Especially, when competing to the top. A true servant will always have compassion on others, they never go with their hands out. They always gain through the sweat of their own brow.

A humble heart God will always hear and so will others. It is not one who goes with their chest out looking down at others. Whoever exalted himself will always be humbled, and whomever humble themselves will be exalted. They are not the ones who point out the faults in others to be exalted. They are not those who frown upon another with a pointing finger. They are not conniving with hidden agendas to inflict pain.

A humble heart will always hear from God and experience Jesus with face-to-face experiences. They are the ones who stand out in a crowd because of this. God says if my people who are called by his name will humble themselves first and pray, seek his face, turn from their wicked ways then they will hear from heaven. (2 Chronicles 7:14)

A humble heart doesn't really have to prove anything. Their God will fight their battles. They are the ones who obey his commands. Honey there is no competition. Just humble your heart and you will get yours.

A Heart Of Stone!

And I will give you a new heart, and a new spirit I will put within you. And I will remove the heart of stone from your flesh and give you a heart of flesh. And I will put my Spirit within you, and cause you to walk in my statutes and be careful to obey my rules.
Ezekiel 36:26-27

Stones are solid and very hard to be broken. Sometimes they are shaped by the controlled removal stone (Volcano's, Mountains, Large Rocks broken). When carved they are made into a form of art or diamond. The instrument used to carve them are the blades of a saw.

One beautiful stone that is always recognized is the diamond. It comes in many forms and are sculpted to shapes that are very unique. There are many types of diamonds and cuts. You really have to be careful in choosing. If you look into a diamond, you can see the heart and how it was designed.

Human hearts are structured and are uniquely formed. The bible says the heart is deceitful above all things, and desperately sick; who can understand it. (Jeremiah 17:2) A warning to the wise, be very careful who you allow to structure your heart. It can be formed to stone.

You can develop a heart of stone in six ways: 1) not allowing God to heal all brokenness. 2) not building solid and godly relationships; 3) through deceit 4) jealousy; 5) hate formed through selfish vindictive motives and 6) denial which prevents God from healing you. It's sad to say sometimes we all experience this type of stone.

Sometimes the stones are so heavy that they are un-moveable. They are set still as land- marks. It takes a bulldozer to lift and sometimes several of people to position themselves to do the work.

When your heart gets to this place of grounded stones, it is very easy to point someone else to be the blame for failures. They strike at the innocent to form their hearts as there's. They murmur and complain about every situation. Their pain is unhidden and you can usually see it in their eyes. They smile when they are hurting. They hold back their tears when told the truth. *(They and Their meaning of a person whose heart is formed as stone.)*

This is when God is calling you to submit unto Him. He wants to heal you from all brokenness. Will you allow him to perform the miracle in your life. Don't you want to be healed from such pain?

Ask Him, say, "Lord please take this heart of mine and fix it. Remove the stone that settled here. Lord, I need you in my life. I cannot make it without you. Help me to trust you with my whole heart. Give me a clean heart and renew the right spirit. The spirit of you. Let me love again like you made me to love through your Holy Spirit. Remove this heart of stone and allow your blood to run through me again. So I can be free from the pain and walk in the obedience of your Word. I want to love you with my whole heart. I want to serve you. Lord remove this heart of stone so that I can be free to experience you in your peace. Lord, remove this heart of stone so that I can hear you again."

GENETICS

This is how you were made

This is how you are structured and formed

This is how you are labeled

They organize you in their minds

In your education

In your career

In your medical records

I don't want to look like you

I don't want to look like them either

I want to look like me

But honey, it's all in your genes

I don't want to act like you, DON'T!

Honey, find you and structure you, it's all up to you.

Start early, fight against weaknesses or make something out of your strengths

Yes, you can be like……….

It all starts with conditioning your mind.

Let's go to the gym

Let's read and learn

Let's put down the bottle

What are you smoking?

Let's together reorganize our life, the promise is yours.

Didn't He promise you a life full of good health, peace of mind?

A life full of abundance?

Honey, it is all in your genes

He's your father and mine.

Can't you see? Look into that mirror and let Him (Christ) shine.

Dear God show my children's children your promises. Teach them never to be ashamed of you and it was never about me (them) but about you. Please get the glory out of their lives? Help me to speak life over their lives? Help me to believe your Word, speak your Word to structure their future? Help me to receive a better life of promises for them and see that my prayers and dreams come true?

Family

JEALOUSY

Set me as a seal upon thine heart, As a seal upon thine arm: For love is strong as death; **Jealousy is cruel as the grave;** *The coals thereof are coals of fire, Which hath a most vehement flame.*
(Song of Solomon 8:1, KJV)

Jealousy is the cruel as the grave. Jealousy kills and destroys every relationship.

How can one identify jealousy?

Jealousy compares with others to show its identity through competition and hate. Jealousy points out others flaws and despairs one's true worth through pride, hurt and deceit.

Jealousy never accepts the truth it always kills with words of hate. It blinds, it chokes out, it divides, it manipulates.

Who needs jealousy when God's unfailing love and heart is big enough for all?

Jealousy creeps in the heart and allows us to speak of the hidden things that crept in through deceit or by being provoked by your enemy (Satan). Who needs jealousy when his promises are so real and for everyone who does not faint to his temptations?

Jealousy will hold back from every promise that God has promised you. It steals every blessing and purpose because of its evil plan for destruction.

It's wicked

It does wicked things.

It blinds the truth.

God loves us all! Why hate on what God has done for us all? Don't you know you are blessed? Join in and Rejoice never envy one another.

Jealousy will not allow you to rejoice with others when they are being blessed.

It's a force from Satan's plan to kill still and destroy. It's that evil eye that is always recognized.

It's a threat and promise for destruction if used.

Jealousy who needs it? Envy who? Not I not you. My relationships are promised to be mended through love and not corruption. Jealousy is the route from the grave.

Let it stay there!

It's a spirit that will not be glorified in the people of God's Kingdom.

MOMMA AND DADDY'S EYES

Your eyes are as bright as the sun above. Who could create something so beautiful and bright? That looks upon the beauty of all creations that shows the hidden sights that no one else sees….

Momma and Daddy's eyes

That knows best, shows best, and lives the best for God's promised

Momma and Daddy's eyes

Tell no lie, shows no one, but loves unconditionally

Momma and Daddy's eyes

Unravels the truth, never reveals it and holds on until the day of victorious moments

Momma and Daddy's eyes

Hidden pride, boasts on God's creation, and never hides

Momma and Daddy's eyes

Know what's best for their creation and makes it happen for their little ones

Momma and Daddy's eyes

Love, protect, nourish, and never neglect

Momma and Daddy's eyes

As beautiful as the sky never dim and always love and look up to every darkened moment for direction from above

Momma and Daddy's eyes

Always wise, wipe away all pain in faith with prayer and supplication, they can never go wrong because their heavenly Father above helps leads through righteousness at all times!

Momma and Daddy's eyes...
Tell no lie!

Children are a bundle of joy, they are of God's creation. It took me a while to mature to the place of happiness when it came to parenthood. I was very scared and did not know how to begin being a parent.

I looked to others for direction and instruction but, there was always a comparison. I really didn't know how to be happy for the miracle God gave me, until God allowed me to see the beautiful daughter He gave me.

I wanted so badly to give her everything that I didn't have in growing up. I didn't shelter her I just tried to show her a better way to look at life. Amazingly, she's wiser than I thought, that's why I praise God for her.

Through her I was able to see God's purpose and love. I was able to dream aloud and help structure the plans for her life. It became difficult at times especially, in her teen-age and young adult years when peers were very important to her.

I tried to tell her not to rush God's plans because he knows her heart desires. We as parents should have a positive influence on our children where they trust us to know end. This way our children will know that we want what's best for them. It only comes through prayer, love, patience, and the right communication in grace.

So, does every child live out their dream? Yes, only the wise and if they can trust who God has created them to be! He knows what's best for them and if they are in a place to listen and hear, they will too. God will lead them to it and form their eyes to see it too.

Grandma's Angel

May 29, 2014

Are they not all ministering spirits sent forth to minister for those who will inherit salvation? (Hebrews 1:14, KJV)

One month ago I encouraged my sister and friend in the Lord in the loss of her dear Grandmother who was about 98 years old. I shared to her my stories of Grandma's Angel. Although, I was taught to never worship angels but to know that they do exist. I shared her of my stories of grandma's angel. She will always be in my heart; her presence, laughter, teachings and corrections of love especially, in times when I'm in the kitchen cooking, gardening, learning and maturing. *"The wise in heart shall be called prudent: and the sweetness of the lips increaseth learning." (Proverbs 16:21)*

Grandma's angel

This morning, I felt your presence even the more as I was meditating, praying, and reading on my deck. When I held my hand to pray, I felt your presence in a gentle touch. As though you were touching and agreeing with me.

Grandma's angel.

Even more than ever before I know that your prayers are still working and mine too! The effectual fervent prayers of the righteous availeth much! As I was praying for peace in my home I experienced it even the more.

Grandma's angel

God revealed to me the many clouds of witnesses that He sends to surround me. To help instruct, lead, guide and direct me, especially the ones to encourage me.

Dear God, thank you for your warring angels, the messengers, ministering angels, and protecting angels.

Most of all thank you for Grandma's Angel.

I had wonderful Grandmothers who were nurturers, prayer warriors, and whose radiance was of peace and love. They feared the Lord and worked very hard for years in the church, instructing and teaching other young ladies on how to become better influential leaders in their homes as wives and mothers. They exemplified faithfulness when it came to their duties as wives, parents, grandparents, and spiritual leaders. They lead by example.

"The heart of the wise teacheth his mouth, and addeth learning to his lips. Pleasant words are as a honeycomb, sweet to the soul, and health to the bones." (Proverbs, 16:23-24, KJV)

Unfortunately, my grandmothers went on to be with the Lord in glory. I was very fortunate to learn from them all the way up to my mid-twenties. I was a young single mother who tried to embrace every teaching that I could hear or remember. Sometimes, pride and youthfulness caused me not to hear but, God allowed me to remember through Grandma's angel.

I am a blessed woman of God who was taught to honor the wise and seek after godly wisdom. I never challenged them nor disrespected them because I was taught not to. They were quiet, bold, good teachers, motivators, and builders too. They can be the ones to keep everything together and at times it would be their gentleness that brings comfort to your heart, reminding you that everything is alright. They are the backbone of the family that keeps everything going.

I would sometimes get a tickle in my stomach to remind me even of the funny times too. I had some great grandmothers and I'm pretty sure you do too. Embrace every moment that God allows them to be in your life because there's no one like them. If it had not been for God and them, your parents could never exist, that means you too.

This is of the main leadership in family that always deserves flowers Great-Grandmothers, Grandmothers, Grandmas, G-Mas, Nana's and Momma 2s.

I love all my grandmothers! Your God-fearing love will always be cherished. May you rest in peace knowing that your loyalty, diligence, prayers, and legacy of faith is still alive. Grandma's Angel is still with me.

SWITCHIN' IN THE KITCHEN

The aromas of fresh pies, cakes, and bakery filled the room as I walked in the kitchen. Nicky come and help me with this dish she said. I replied, "I know nothing about baking I never had the gift." No one told you about switchin' in the Kitchen. I laughed, and replied, "No Grandma."

Switchin' in the Kitchen

She placed an apron on me and told me to follow her instructions

First wash your hands

Then she went to explain the recipes of life

If you want to get his attention start Switchin' in the kitchen

A way to a man's heart is through his stomach

Switchin in the kitchen

Always follow a good recipe

Measure every ingredient and sometimes if you have to add a little spice to it to make the taste to your liking, by all means do it with love

A little here and a little there

Never serve your guest without tasting your dish first

And when you're done always clean up after yourself

The rules of the kitchen

In a very high pitched voice she sang, "Switchin in the Kitchen."

A very wise woman she was, a woman after God's own Heart explained the basic rules of the kitchen, the ingredients of life. Within a decade of these instructions this woman went to be with the Lord. It would be lessons like these that prepared me for my future that I will always embrace, cherish, and pass on. She was not physically there at my wedding but her spirit of love has always been there.

The Silent Whispers Will Always Be Cherished

The silent whispers will always be cherished

The whispers of guidance and instructions, the hidden laughter and chuckles

The very soft words with a southern slang of sassiness to correct with love will always be remembered

Your prayers were different than mine you used the sign of the cross

Does that mean that your faith was not as strong as mine?

I always saw your concern in that sign that showed God's love through you.

The silent whispers will always be cherished

As I watched you when you could not voice your heart's concern

I knew that your love was so dear and your innocence was still there

Words as, "That was so nice" allowed me to see that you cared

Even when you could not say it your eyes did, to allow us to know that your soul was still there

Also, the time when you place your finger over your mouth to sign quiet

I saw the angel who was there

The squeezing of the hands and the kicking of your feet expressed to us that you were yet aware

Your silent whispers will always be cherished because I know that they were so sincere!

The silent whispers will always be cherished.

"It is estimated that as many as 5.1 million Americans may have Alzheimer's disease. About a half million Americans younger than age 65 have some form of dementia, including Alzheimer's disease. It is also estimated that one to four family members act as caregivers for everyone with Alzheimer's disease." (AFA)

A LITTLE BOY WHO NEVER LISTENS

A little boy who never listens and runs

He knows all, speaks all, and tells everyone right from wrong and never sees wrong in himself

Is he running from himself?

Is the hurt so strong that it causes bitterness and strong holds of pain that are so self –inflicting that it inflicts everyone else?

What is he hearing in his head?

Who is it?

Is it God?

Is it Jesus?

The quiet screams and the loud shouts

Who is it that he trusts?

The swinging emotions that were never healed

A heart with broken pieces with no shield

The silent cries and hidden tears

Little boy cry out aloud to your heavenly Father spare not for he knows your pain, he sees your tears, and deepest hearts concern. He knows your desires. He knows your fears.

He will never lead you astray

Little boy come forth with full strength

Little Boy, Young Man, Man of God will you listen?

Come forth and listen and be obedient to hear

Will you submit to your heavenly Father's commands?

Let go of pride and follow me sayeth the Lord of Hosts

The little boy who never listens hear the words of wisdom

Listen!

BIG BROTHER

Let love be without dissimulation. Abhor that which is evil; cleave to that which is good. Be kindly affectionate one to another with brotherly love; in honor preferring one another. John 13:31-35, KJV

Tall in stature, strong you are big brother is what I call you

My big brother runs very fast; he's swift around the corners and courageous when it comes to each challenge

God-fearing man he is and charmer as well

He hides his emotions and builds up everyone else's

Quiet at times but, never let it fool you because he's a thinker and planner too

He's been my strength when I'm weak and let me know it was me being strong

He builds up, never tears down even in his correction he shares it through wisdom

What can I say to a Big Brother when I see him soring high above every mountain that is in his way?

I would say Big Brother where you at? You want me to help you get them out of your way? I would find that bat or I would kneel down and pray. Lord help, my Big Brother get those mountains out of his way. I would remind him of his strength along each pathway.

My big brother that I never knew my big brother who had come along life's journey and pathway. The one I searched for and could not find to fight my battles came along this way. He lifted me when I was down, he pushed me when I had no strength, he was patient to teach when I didn't understand, and he watched me when I was unaware.

My big brother to whom I look up to

My big brother who I dearly miss

My big brother who I will never let anyone mistreat

My big brother who I will always trust

My big brother

My big brother the leader, the man after God's own heart

My big brother the teacher and instructor when everything is falling apart

My big brother with wisdom, good knowledge, and strength

My big brother!

I had only one birth brother and he was younger than me. We are close in age. It was like we were twins, but we fought each other, challenged each other, competed with one another and I really didn't know why? He always had to show his strength over mine. Although, I was older he was taller and the male who was taught to be the leader and he is. I guess it was pride.

Even though we were always at each other's neck challenging one another we would find ourselves defending each other. I wanted so much to be free from my brother's shadow and never really knew how to appreciate him and his purpose of being my brother. The joys of brotherly and sisterly spats would always ring through the hallways of our home.

After maturing I realize that my brother has always been with me. I've been aware to notice his ways to defend and protect me even when we are hundreds of miles in distance from each other. God has allowed me to know his purpose as my baby brother but, tall in stature in my life. My Big Brother!

I later, was able to have big brothers who God placed in my life whether it was through my sister's marriages, through church, and my own marriage. It was a blessing because I started off with one and God granted me more than 20 that I can respect as who they are, my big brother's.

Part of this poem tells about the one that passed away too soon. He was genuine, a charmer, and very non-chalet but, God allow me to understand him and to build a solid brother-sister relationship. I loved my

Big Brother.

I know of a bible story of brothers who could not get along their names were Cain and Able. The relationship of jealousy, envy, and strife killed the other (Able.) It was for prestige and power. It is a generation that causes death of men from the beginning of time. There is a purpose, that God is calling forth of men, that needs to be fulfilled.

He is calling forth men of honor who are warriors; lovers of God, who are peace makers and know how to love others unselfishly. He's calling forth true men, who are humble; yet strong in their faith. He's calling forth true men; who knows their purpose, to be pillars, builders, and leaders. Good examples of men who are my big brothers who God has chosen to be strong men (not weak), who is rooted and stable in God's word. Who are real when it comes to their manhood, God is calling forth Big Brothers.

SISTERLY LOVE

For all this I considered in my heart even to declare all this that the righteous, and the wise, and their works, are in the hand of God: no man knoweth either love or hatred by all that is before them. -Ecclesiastes 9: 1, KJV

Either love or hate! Am I my sister's keeper? Do I live in the shadow of? Can I see her worth or even know her worth? To compare myself with or to look down at because of past hurts; is this sisterly love that I can identify? The beauty queen, the career woman, the mother, the wife....

Our many different identities of shapes and shades of colors cannot describe our uniqueness. Was it really our breast size? In who eyes? Love is patient love is blind. Sisterly love is hard to come by, especially when there is so much un-forgiveness and forces to choose a side. Playing the tug of war with our faith and not even knowing our self-worth. This type cannot hide.

The outer beauty does not show her inner. Life's paths of hurts, struggles, bitterness, and grief can only describe where her strength comes from. Can we reject her because of the unknown or because of hidden jealousies that cannot be described? Does she see what I see? Will I un-cover her secrets because of what???

I want to be me and not her! I want my own identity and want to be me! Can you hear her cries? She's fat, she's skinny, and she cannot fit in my jeans. Can I scream! She just thinks she's all that! It's always been about her…Sisterly love who knows this type?

Is it the kind that I describe? She does not know her own self-worth? Who formed her heart to see with such pain? Was it the comparison too that allowed her to go astray? For what? That's mine not yours.... The many different fights to become who we are, the competition who is the beauty queen, Am I you and are you me? Will I ever be? What really beautifies us? Sisterly love!

To be in the shadow of such beauty and so wise, my sister the challenges that brought you to the beautiful, wise, and mature woman you are today.

My sister I see your growth from birth. My sister whom I love so much! My sister who I will go to war for! My sister whose strength is so strong! My sister whose heart is so brave! My sister who is so sweet and dear! My sister you are so worth more!

My sister, we've cried, we've fought, we've ran, we've prayed, we've conquered, we've changed, we've achieved, we are blessed and not cursed! My sister, do you really know your worth? My big sister, my little sister never let anyone tell you any different. Do you know who you are? You are my sister? The mahogany, light skinned, brown skinned sister that you are. The curly hair, nappy hair, the blue eyed, the green eyed, and brown eye sister you are. No one will come in between this type of love. My sister, she is loved.

Sisterly Love!

Mama's Kitchen

Don't you go in mama's kitchen rearranging her cupboards unless you are adding more to her stash of food that brings forth her recipes of love.

There's so much pride in family recipes that are passed down from generations to generations in Mama's Kitchen.

No one really knows the spices that make everything so right

Humble pies, dressings, macaroni and cheese,

is what I was raised on and no one did cook quite like Mama

Was it because it was Mama's Kitchen?

Dinners could never be done fast enough, I would always be the one to taste her cooking because she never served unless it was to the perfection of my tasting

This was my Mama's Kitchen

No one could come into Mama's Kitchen telling her that her cooking was not right

She put pride in every stroke of mixing and stirring until every ingredient was entered to make her food taste to its delight.

Hidden recipes from her shelves and her book of love

Everyone loves her cooking because it's her home cooking

Meals of soul and delicate dishes

Where the party at, is it in Mama's Kitchen?

Breads, molds, pies, greens, black eyed peas, red beans and rice, gumbo, fried chicken, baked chicken, spaghetti, anyone want Chinese?

My Mama's kitchen is the best kitchen to explain the hidden recipes of life!

Who dances, sings, and prays in the kitchen?

Whispers of laughter, angels of love...

Only in my

Mama's Kitchen

One of my favorite dishes was Shepard's Pie. It was a dish that my parents made when the cupboards were bare and little money left after the bills were paid. Although, we were a blessed family, we still had our struggles with the economy and gaining economic position in life. My parents were really hard workers. This particular dish, was my brother and I favorite.

One day my brother and I asked my parents what the name of the dish was. My dad laughed and said, "Humble Pie." This dish lasted two or three days before pay day. It's something how children knew when pay day was in the home. If we were good and did our chores we experienced an increase too.

I'VE SEEN THE TEARS YOU SHED

Momma's cry. Momma's pain. Momma's tears.

You prayed all night long. Crying aloud to God. I never could understand how to help. I just prayed to Jesus asking Him to help my Momma and to heal her from her pain.

I heard the report that the doctors gave you and that man in church said to you, "whose report will you believe?" Don't you serve our God who heals thee?

I've seen the tears that you shed when you didn't have the money to pay the rent for the month, praying to Jehovah Jireh our Provider. I whispered a prayer asking Jesus to make a way. Telling everyone what Jesus can….and He did.

I've seen the tears that you shed when they broke your heart and left you alone but you were not alone. I saw your angels standing there.

I've seen the tears that you shed when your enemies came in like a flood and you reminded God of his deliverance power saying, "God you promise to never leave me nor forsake me and you would deliver me from this storm!" Unaware of the time and what storm I still believed in God's delivering power. Lord release your waring angels on my mother's behalf. Don't you hear her cry?

I've seen the tears you shed when you heard of the many murders, mistreatment, and the sufferings of the innocent. Praying to God, "Lord free your people from such harm and to protect them from their enemies."

Didn't you say those who sow tears shall reap in shouts of joy? (Psalms 126:5)

I've seen the tears you shed, your precious oils during long prayers, your faith, and your joys; and know that Momma's cry helped pave a way for me.

"Cry aloud do not hold back; lift up your voice like a trumpet; declare to my people their transgression; to the house of Jacob their sins." (Isaiah 58:1)

I Have A Momma Who Are You?

Reminded by a child in the rebellious stage of life. Who thinks that he/she no longer needs guidance or instruction and somehow had gained the trust of their parents. They are now wise and have paved a way for their futures with disrespecting rulers, teachers, leaders such as religious leaders, their parents, elders, and authorities.

One day I saw my neighbor's child do something out of the ordinary that I knew that would send harm his way. I warned as if he was my child with instructions that would pave his way for his future or career. He looked at me as if he was to respond, I have a Momma, who are you?

Another day I saw a very close friend of my child's headed down a road of destruction of promiscuity and shame. I told him not to go down that road and explained in detailed why. I told him of a better future ahead if he stayed focused. He replied, "I have a Momma who are you?"

Child what does your future look like? Woman I'm sorry you cannot tell me how to live my life have you seen yours? But, young man/young woman yes I have. Can you not fall in the same traps? You are not my momma you cannot tell me what to do! I have a Momma who are you?

Stop thinking everyone is you, I heard a young lady reply in her growing pains. Honey I see your future. It is so bright; will you not combat with Godly instructions? You cannot tell me what to do! I have a mother who are you?

I am no one, this woman replied, just a messenger sent by God to guide. How dare this old woman tell me this is not my season yet? I thought she was supposed to be in my corner somewhere trusting God in prayer. She talks too much! I have a Momma who are you?

Do you adopt children of this kind? Who are their parents? They said what? I have a Momma who are you?

I pray for all mothers whose child have come to this place of identity needing no guidance or wisdom. They are the teachers who do not need teachers. They are the lawyers who have no education. They are the business men and women who have their own businesses in High School. They are the doctors who have no practice at age 2. Saying, "I'm grown I don't need a momma like you." I am the momma who are you.

SOCIETY

WHO AM I?

Who am I?

Am I who I am behind my weave?

The color of my hair

Does it make me, me?

Am I who I am because of my shape?

My bra size or my jean size does that make me who I am?

Is it my curves in my hips, the fullness of my lips, the curls in my locks that make me who I am?

Am I my mother's child or my daddy's heart?

Am I me behind them?

Is it my skin color that makes me me?

Or is it the rhythms behind the beat when I dance that make me? Who I am?

Am I that smile, that light up the room and glows in dark places?

Is that me?

Or am I the one who hides in the corner so fearful of one's perception of me?

Am I that one that takes on every challenge and come out victorious because I am that overcomer?

Who am I?

Am I you

Or Am I me?

I am who I am.

I am who sent me to you

All that God created me to be!

MY BEST FRIEND...

What is a best friend to a man or woman?

Is it someone you hang out with daily to shout the breeze and talk about the ladies?

What is a best friend to a woman? Is it someone who you trust and have confidence in? The one who knows the inner most secrets with?

I really couldn't tell you that a best friend is one you cherish or love, especially when friendship is dependent upon man, woman, or your favorite toy or animal.

The days, the months, the years, and decades between the times one shares.

The laughter, the tears, and the time in prayer

Can I say you were not there? Not at all!

The tough times throughout the years of growing

The heartaches, the pain, and every cry for help

Were you there?

My best friend for years was dependent upon the comfort of knowing you were there.

When I am afraid, alone, in my quiet times, toiling, and warring times you were there.

Who is a best friend?

Is it I?

Is it you?

Is it my sister, my brother?

Is it my mom or dad?

Is it my husband or wife?

My dog Benji?

Is it Jesus?

Is it who?

My best friend, thank you for never leaving me alone and teaching me the importance of loyalty and trust. You have always been there.

Don't Judge Me

Don't judge me because I see the natural beauty that others don't see

The darkness of your skin, the red in your lips and your bright white teeth that light up every room that you're in,

God's wonderful master piece being formed in his likeness

Don't judge Me when others can't hear what I hear

A child's cry and longing to be accepted and fit in a society that has been cultivated to a style of hate and ugliness that was not meant for God's purpose of formality

Don't judge me when I can't understand the bitter stones that you throw because of your own hurt and pain.

Don't judge me when I see that there's a pathway of escape for the ones tormented for years of not being accepted in a society that has blinded their eyes for the unknown.

Don't judge me when you can't hear what I say because of the blocks of pride that closed your ears from the hidden things

The riddles to my rhymes the beats to my heart that rocks to every bass line.

Don't judge me when my skin is light and loves to change with the sun light or if I have red tones that highlights my freckles.

Don't judge me when I can wear a weave, some braids, a natural, or twists in my hair and still bring about a style that will move all heads.

Don't judge me or turn me a way because I'm still trying to find life's pathways from financial bondages due to the many doors closed in my face.

Don't judge me when I finally found the mysteries of God's purpose for my life and I'm running with it.

Don't judge me because I have been given a chance to tread upon the waters and look to blue skies, sunshine, and the rain that falls. His faith has driven me,

That's the son too. I see the sparkles and light that only He shines.

Don't judge me!

IF I WERE THE PRESIDENT FOR A YEAR

If I were the President of the United States for one year I would address the racism and prejudice issues that are yet alive in our country. I would discuss the factors hidden and never justified when it comes to racial identity, cultures, and classification. Our nation is still struggling with inferiority issues and fears especially when it comes to confidence and trust.

I would support every issue with the Christianity faith and the Word of God; focusing on brotherly and sisterly love. I would also elevate the strong beliefs of mankind and how to keep the brotherhood going. "Honor all men, love the brotherhood, fear God and honor the King." (1 Peter 2:17).

If I were the President of the United States for one year I would address the issues that we as a nation cannot identify, because of how the new world has structured culture and beliefs. Or was it the old world first? We have come a long way from the 1900's and the Civil Rights Movement but yet, we have become adapted and relaxed to a system that has not worked for years.

I would address the fears of circular affects with history repeating itself when it comes to the right person for the job in a multi-cultural society. Does anyone know about love? Where is Christ in all these Christians? Is it all about power? Who is gaining here?

The hidden prejudice of secret societies that hold people from reaching their American Dream, it should never be anyone's size, shape or color that would not keep them from achieving this dream. It should never be about race, religious beliefs, or your socio-economic status for you to be heard.

Our world is formed of many colors, race, religion, and beliefs; but the silent is being heard. Is it really the color that makes us competitive with one another or the dollar? Is it our race that identifies us? Is it our creed? It can be if it's structured around evil, wickedness, and hate. The insecurities that one struggles with should not make him inferior to their brother? Love conquers all!!!

I believe that everyone is different and unique. One cannot be identified as who they are without really having knowledge of what type of person they are. Who has courage to believe, to be identified by race, culture, religion or economic classification would be the new I.D.'s that we would have to carry and present to whoever that's in charge? Yet, that too still will give people the right to choose and that can be a fine line of discrimination. Minority? Majority? What is unity? Will there ever be strength?

Diversity is the key when it comes to building and creating new. One's strong belief should never make one inferior to the other. People are to embrace the good and work on the bad. That only comes through effective leadership that exemplifies true love. Trust God and not evil! In God, we have the faith to believe!

To kill someone because of your fear or because of what you read or heard has been the old history that we don't want to ever relive. Let's make new! Everyone is not alike. Because of that do we run from, hate others, and project a defensive nature, because, of your skin color or beliefs? Why snatch away God's purpose? What is your biggest fear? Is it you? Is it that you'll never conquer or achieve? You won't if you're always looking for the reflection of you?

If I were president for one year I would speak to a nation and instruct them to build never tear down, promote good health wealth and peace of mind. I will justify every social order, civil issue, world matters with moral order that works to edify and build a solid nation of wealth through, the Jesus Christ type of love!

Humankind should not be classified by someone else's emotions. Your race, your religion, your beliefs, your color, and socio-economic standards do classify who you are. It does not justify you though. Justification only comes through the love of God. "There is no fear in love; but perfect love casteth out fear: because fear hath torment. He that feareth is not made perfect in love. (1 John 4:7) Don't hate me because I love me. Believe that Jesus Christ is the Man of God, I am unique, and I am an American citizen, are you? If I were president for one year? Humm?

LIKE A WHIRLWIND

Have you ever been in a whirlwind twisting around and around barely seeing where you're going and all you can hear are the screams and cries of the hearts of people who are so dear?

Getting caught up in their issues never knowing how to solve every given problem

Tormented by the sounds that, would cause anyone to fear.

Weathering the storms that takes your breath away taking you places where no one ever has been

Like a whirlwind?

Repeating cycles of generations…

Pride, hate, and despair

Laughter's, screams, and tears

Bullying, teasing, fighting

Lies, excuses, and cheats

Pain, sorrows, and can I holler…

Help me Lord please

Like a whirlwind with no direction no guidance no assistance

Who can I trust? Is it man that I put my confidence in?

Going through the circles of life climbing every mountain crossing every dry desert never seeing through the sand and can I say the darkness in my eyes has no shadows?

Where is the light?

It's like a whirlwind

Like Dorothy in the Land of Oz

Strange things happening before your eyes and never knowing if it's God or Satan

Where are the angels from above?

Who's judging me now?

What? Say God's Word you say

How can I remember His Word or His promises in such areas of darkness?

Mocking's, rattling in my ears

They are all contradicting God's truth according to my life can you hear?

Confusion only comes from Satan

Is that you God in those people? Humph?

Like a whirlwind

Getting trapped in

Not knowing how to get out

Over worked, under paid, un-respected and does anyone knows who gets the honor here?

God, you said you would never put more on me than I could bare

You said that weeping may endure for a night and joy comes in the morning

And here comes that hand pulling you out

Wew!

Strength from above twisting and turning placing you to a still

Then calming the winds sets in

A great sound of gladness you start to hear

Love and joy starts filling the atmosphere

A shining star from above appears and you can see your path so clear

Your future is great my dear

No more sorrows and your joys for tomorrow is so near

You can see the sun (Son) so clear

Feeling its warming touch

Sounds of comfort starts to whisper in your ear

Saying the storm is over now it's your season walk into your new year

Like a whirlwind

Or a bad dream turning good

God will quiet your storms and bring forth His promises hidden in his Word

If you stand still

He will bring you out and unfold the truth and ease your pain

And bring you through every whirlwind

No more dizziness, no more sorrows

Prayers are answered and the path of righteousness is so straight

You can see where you're going, the roads are golden

Success begins to happen

Dreams are fulfilled and you are known for your accomplishments

Like a whirlwind

Thank you, Evangelist Deborah Walton, and the Women Advance (The Agape Jurisdiction) for the prophecies and prayers given from the Holy Spirit through true Women of God.

SET ME FREE!

When I sit around and view my circumstances and wonder how I can come out of such depression, my heart wants to cry set me free!

I want so bad for them to see how I see them free. Don't they see poverty is still yet alive? Don't they see that they too can be free!

There are people whose lives are depended on every substance that allows Satan's demons to overtake their minds.

All they have time to be is idled about theirs and others. Don't they have time to dream aloud and pray? Why ponder on others when you can stand on God's Word and believe?

You have children, they hear you and are watching. Can't you see? They move on your emotions and actions. Is it time to see that they too can be free?

Your children know no different and they are screaming inside to set them free! Parents wisen up. Don't you see they are masterpieces in the making? Can't you see that they have a dream?

Free from oppression, free from distractions, free from poverty, free from ignorance, free from words of hate, free from a dying world, free from you, free from me

Set me free

When I'm free I would be able to see, all what God intended me to be

When I'm free I can understand and recognize everything? Only what He wants me to see!

When I'm free my mind is elevated on those things that are above

When I'm free I can love again because I'm free to be who he intended me to be

Set me free

Free to dance

Free to laugh

Free to be me

Free to be you

Set them all free.

PRESS THROUGH YOUR DISTRACTIONS

Distraction, "A thing that prevents someone from giving full attention of something else. The extreme agitation of the mind or emotion."

Have you ever been interrupted throughout the day and try to stay on task with every given deadline? The phone rings, there's questions to be answered, home calls, children call, husband calls, boss needs you to stay on task. These, my friend, are distractions.

How about the kind of distractions that comes when you are so very focused, trying to accomplish a dream or goal? They can come through a sound, woman, or man. They are never expected.

They through you off of the track and sometimes pull you to the back of the line because they have to come first. They are very self-centered, careless, and self-motivated.

A distract mindset will come when you are in the middle of a sentence, rather talking or writing they will come.

While trying to complete a goal they come to procrastinate you or stop you from your achievements.

Distractions are not your friend they are your worst enemy. They are the ones who run you down to cut in front of you to achieve their goal to stop, hinder, overtake, and conquer you.

When they come, you have to press through!

Press through the mind wandering moments, the mind washer habitats, and the agitations that cause frustration.

Press through when you feel like giving in and throwing in the towel because of time will not permit you to reach every given deadline.

Press through when you hear the laughter and mockery from your competitors and bullies. Press through every challenge, every struggle, every disappointment, every heart, and every pain.

Press through your distractions.

GOSSIP
Who Told You? How Do You Know?

He who guards his mouth and his tongue keeps himself from trouble.
-Prov. 21:23, KJV

Thou should not go up and down as a talebearer among thy people: neither shalt thou stand against the blood of thy neighbor: I am the Lord. Thou shalt not hate thy brother in thy heart: thou shalt in any wise rebuke thy neighbor, and not suffer sin upon them. Thou shalt not avenge, nor bear any grudge against the children of thy people, but thou shalt love thy neighbor as thyself: I am the Lord
-Leviticus 19:16-18, KJV

Girl did you know that…? Let me tell you my friend who's her third or fourth cousin told me and I trust her because we've been friends over 15 years.

Gossip you hear tales of other people's stories that formed the heart of a stranger who really don't know.

You hear it in the office, in school on the play-ground, and Lord have mercy should I say it… in church too.

It's a sin to tear apart a person's character without even knowing them.

Hello, do you know me? Or what have you heard through the grapevine today?

A perfect person trying to live in a perfect world or should I say

A person striving for perfection trying to find acceptance

Who told you? How do you know?

Do you have your facts right or are you just going by hearsay?

Didn't you know that hearsay was a little loss lad trying to find their direction

Out of my life on a path of finding their own business

Gossip is a sin

Did Jesus say it? How do you know?

Find a book talk about what you learned

Find a puzzle and try to put it back together again

Find a loss soul and see how it got loss could it be you?

Who told you? How do you know?

How do you know that person who could have been someone very special in their children's eyes, didn't you know? Don't you even care?

Your labeling is not really in disguise

It's a fine line of blasphemy because God said they are special.

Do you really know their story or are you going by what you heard?

Chains of words being twisted

Satisfying the lust of someone else's large chest that has labeled you HAUGHTY, NAUGHTY, and hiding from their own hidden stories...

Don't you have something better to do than to sit around and talk up, tangle up, and shoot the breeze?

There's not enough time in a day

I'm too busy to worry about what they say aren't you?

Did you tell them about Jesus?

Tell who?

You know those who told you about that person

Who?

Who started this gossip anyway and why?

How do you know who told you?

Never repeat something that someone confides in you about

You may start a war unaware

That had your name written all over it

Did you know how to pray?

Don't you have any compassion?

Empathy, sympathy, or agape love

That's what you're missing

Girl I know that's right because it's the truth!

WHO OFFENDED YOU?

He who covers and forgives an offense seeks love, but he who repeats and harps on a matter separates even closes friends.
-Proverbs 17:9 AMP

When someone is offended, they find themselves in a deep combative conversation

Whether it's aimed directly at a person amongst friends and family

or in confrontation giving a person a piece of their mind.

My question is to you, who offended you?

Offense is a source of un-forgiveness

It allows you to ponder on words, and harvest those that are directed towards you

It forms one's heart to bitter and cold

Because of, the abundance of the heart the mouth speaks

Somebody needs to be praying

Don't you know that there is death and life in the power of the tongue?

Saints can't you hear, you have power!

Offense starts wars

Offense never covers one's faults; it uncovers which is very unwise

It attacks one's character and not even innocence is protected

It's an ignorant way of living

Who has offended you?

It separates family and friends

It causes no one to want to be around you because all you do is talk about those who hurt you or offended you.

Who has offended you?

Offense will cause one to become distant, secluded, and alone.

It causes an evil emotion of defense

Didn't you know that no weapon formed against you shall prosper?

Didn't you know that God will fight your every battle….

No longer do you have to change your character to defend you from your offenders

No longer do you have to become Dr. Jeckle and Mr. Hide or Sybil

No longer will you have to become your hater's punching bag for their bad day

No longer will you have to be accused of someone else's anger or hidden emotion

Take charge! Be bold and aware of Satan's devices

You have a protector and He will send His army of angels to fight every battle.

Don't be offended, walk in forgiveness, and pray for the spirit of truth that always causes Satan's bait to fail.

Who has offended you?

GOD GIVE ME A MILLION SO I CAN BE FREE!

Is money the answer to all problems? You would think. I wouldn't know because it's something I never had.

Some people flaunt it and others hide it. I, for one, would try to make something out of it.

God give me a million so I can be free!

Free from bills, free from debt, free from poverty, and free from my accusers blaming me…

I would pay them all back! Who likes to be depressed? Owing the world, family, and friends. Didn't the Bible say owe no man any good thing?

God please free me….

Free from guilt, free from shame, free from almost going insane.

Free from my enemies

Do you think money would make them shut-up?

Free from torment

Do you think money is the answer to all problems?

God give me a million so I can be free

Did I hear, play the lottery? My money is spent before some lottery…it is too precious to me.

I heard someone say the more you have the more you spend. Is it true?

Or learn how to manage what you have?

The rich get richer and poor get poorer.

I thought you said the wealth of wicked is laid up for the righteous?

God Give Me A Million So I Can Be Free!

WHY HAVE YOU MADE ME YOUR ENEMY?

...You have heard that it was said, 'YOU SHALL LOVE YOUR NEIGHBOR and hate your enemy.' But I say to you, love your enemies and pray for those who persecute you, so that you may be sons of your Father who is in heaven; for He causes His sun to rise on the evil and the good, and sends rain on the righteous and the unrighteous.... Matthew 5:44

Hello, what did I do now? Was it how I looked today? Was it what I said? Stop screaming at me! I've done nothing wrong!

It was your error not mine? Why point at me when you are wrong? Why have you made me your enemy?

Why are you so angry? What have your emotions in such an up roar? All I said was hello? And you replied in a grudging way with sighs of hate…Hi! Did it hurt you to reply?

Forcing others to be like you and stirring their eyes and heart to see like you. Sister girl don't you know you are loved? Why have you made me your enemy?

I see your hidden tears and know your worries. Is it that you do not want the truth to be told? You are hurting inside. Let me pray for you.

Don't you know the power of prayer will turn away wrath, lift all heavy loads and make your burdens light? Child, I promise you, it is not all about you.

Why is your face and eyes so red? Why have you made me your enemy? Come on, let's pray. That's alright I will pray for you.

I have so much to overcome and achieve in life. I have places to go and goals to meet. Please join me or get out of my way because I am not your enemy. You are!

Let us together allow God to fulfill His promises or get out of the way of what God is doing. You are not my enemy. You are your own. I love you and will continue to pray for you.

Why have you made me your enemy?

I'M JUST A NEGRA AS YOU?

For I say, through the grace given unto me, to every man that is among you, not to think of himself more highly than he ought to think; but to think soberly, according as God hath dealt to every man the measure of faith. Romans 12:3, KJV

Reflecting on a high yellow little girl with curly long braids. One day this little girl went to school acknowledging who she was as an individual. She was mistreated by her peers with teasing, laughing, bullying, mockery, and needless to say she was even spat on. This little girl never knew why.

She would try to befriend the Caucasian classmates and they disliked her because of her skin color, slang, and curly hair. She tried to befriend her African-American classmates and they mistreated her because of what her parents made her to be.

One day while in class she was sitting at her desk and her classmate who was of the same nationality took her hair and placed it in black ink and wrote with it. She turned around and snatched her braid and said with a very strong tone, "I'm Just a Negra as You."

This story has <u>impressed</u> upon my heart to write to this little girl who really didn't know why people were so mean to her. She struggled just like all the rest to find her place in society, a very smart and intelligent young lady who stood about 4"1" tall. Her integrity was struck by others who labeled her as not having a brain in her head (Having knowledge, common sense, dreams, and goals).

Did this young girl meet her dreams? Was her fight not strong enough? Was it her anger that kept her at a standstill in life? Her cry for help was never heard because of the strength of people who kept her quiet. What happened to her faith? What happened to her power?

All the other Negro students could <u>strive</u> above most because of their height or was it because of their combative nature to steal from and keep small giants down? They could achieve, go places in life, dream and conquer. They stole words, ideas, and said it was theirs.

Watching all the others Negro students find their place in society, she never found hers. Is it because she was struck the wrong way in that fight? Was it because she wasn't as black as others? Was it because she wasn't as light as others?

It wasn't her fault that her hair was curly or her braids were so long. It wasn't her fault that her skin had a high yellow or red tone. It wasn't she that made herself. This little girl probably questioned God asking him why was she hated and mistreated so badly by her peers?

She was never the type to go asking people to like her or "Would you be my friend?" She was the little tall girl who stayed the humbled servant. Who worked hard to graduate and become the person God made her to be. A stubborn girl she is. Can you hear her soft words or loud screams?

Did anyone know her heart or hear her dreams? Did she strive above many to believe? Did she stay seated never standing or did she walk into her destiny? She is just as Negra as you? Make room for her please.

Inspired by story told by My Great Auntie Cora.

There are many crimes but Black on Black Crime makes my skin curl.

AMERICA THE HOME OF THE FREE

"Over 1,400 more black Americans murdered other blacks in two years than were lynched from 1882 to 1968." (Briebart, 2015)

My country tis of the sweet land of liberty of thee I sing

Land where my fathers died Land of the pilgrim's pride. From every mountain side Let Freedom Ring!

God show me a mountain so that I can climb

Reaching to the top praying in every step

Landing screaming free at last free at last thank God Almighty I'm free at last!

Am I home?

Is this America?

Is this the place where my family fought for my freedom?

World War I, World War II, the Korean War, Vietnam, Racial Wars, the Gulf, and Middle Eastern Wars?

The place they built monuments and worked for their generations to come.

A place where people are free to be who they are

Americans

Costumed and cultured to be free

Americans

Free to ignore or love thy neighbor as thyself

Where music has cultivated a life for living

What genre do you like?

Where careers are at wide range and molded us to leadership

Is this America where education is hard to come by or is it?

My country tis of the sweet sweet land of liberty

Where my identity shows my authority through justice for all

My country,

America

From every mountain side let freedom RING!

CAN I BE JUST AN AMERICAN AS YOU?

"The American Dream is that dream of a land in which life should be better and richer and fuller for everyone, with opportunity for each according to ability or achievement." Reflections from James Truslow Adams, Epic of America. "Whom the Son sets free is free indeed." (John 8:36, KJV)

I don't know if my people came over to America on a ship,

If they were sold into slavery working hard to survive.

I don't know what hardships led me to desire the big dream

Was it looking at you?

Can I be just an American as you?

Free from bondage free from enslaved mindsets

Free from ignorance

Where is this land?

Years of searching falling into the traps of sins that we call freedom.

Is it actually freedom?

I want free education

I want a career

I want a family

I want to live my dream with a big house, a car, and a dog.

I want freedom and liberty to believe in one God

I want to be able to achieve and excel to the highest accomplishments of life.

I want favor and grace

I want to be free to pray always and never faint

I want to be able to choose just like you.

Can I be just an American as You?

POWER!

White Power Black Power Man Power Girl Power what about the Holy Ghost Power!

Power is a strong word. Power is the ability to achieve, to excel, to endure, and to do almost anything. Some gain it through people, social groups, organizations, cultures, race, colors, genders, and most of all God. Once gained it's something one would never want to lose.

We were here first

We owned crops and land

We had education before you even came over to our country

White Power

Come on let's show our strength

Said a very mixed white American who was German, Polish, and Italian.

I'm sorry weren't you or your family apart of the immigration move too? What made you fit in the crowd?

Who gave you favor? Was it your lies that they trust? Any and everything goes, especially when you are in control. Whose Power?

Together we stand, divided we fall.

Am I my brother's keeper?

Brother meaning Black Brother or Black Sister?

Will I cover your faults and take the fall? Or together we stand for the Power we deserve?

No longer will we be struck down because of someone else's pride.

Don't you let them know who or where your strength comes from

Black Power!

Yes, we are smart and together we can be strong. Without us men are weak. We have the compassion and love that you need. We stand strong to build and create. We are precious, we are unique, beautiful, charismatic, and yes, wise. Our caring nature set the mood for any room and will move the emotions of those who will listen. We can handle just about anything, we are multi-taskers, we are super girls and wonder women on any given day.

Girl Power!

The world is structured by you. You are leaders made to lead. Together building, creating, and strengthening. You rule through decisions. Your pride is built on your ego and no one stands to tear you down unless you let them. Our world was built on your strength. If anyone stands between you and power you show your strength through…

Man Power!

But what is the power that we all need as White, Black, Asian, Mexican, Indian, female (girl), male (man) to withstand to love to build, to create, to be lead, to be consoled, to be who we are as individuals in a world who do not know Christ in the beauty of his holiness?

What power

Gives us unity and strength?

What power

Gives us love and compassion?

What power

Shows us our futures and grants us grace to gain it?

What power gives us confidence and boldness?

What power gives us holy character with the fruit of his spirit?

It is the Holy Ghost Power!

Why not gain it all with His power!

Together we have the power.

Don't Weaken Me So You Can Be Strong!

Who by faith conquered kingdoms performed acts of righteousness, obtained promises, shut the mouth of lions, quenched the power of fire, escaped the edge of the sword, from weakness were made strong, became mighty in war, put foreign armies to flight. Hebrews 11: 33-34

Don't shallow my character with words of hate so that you can be strong.

Forming parties through social events and gossip sessions

Getting pulled in to organizations through lured communications for someone else's political gain.

Don't weaken me so that you can be strong!

Didn't you know I was wiser than that?

How dare you get caught up in the game?

Didn't you know we are in an apocalyptic battle in one country between parties, religions, cultures, race, sex, nationalities?

And you want to weaken me so you can be strong?

People are dying because of someone else's weakness

And you want to point out my flaws for more political gain?

Muffle my words, twist up the meanings, scream out my name, blaming me for your mess-ups.

Don't you see who's weak here?

You make us all look bad!

I'm sorry dear you make yourself look bad.

You had the power to give back to someone else's strength.

You've pushed me too far with my back against the wall

I still will have strength screaming Jesus!

With power from up high releasing his angels in my defense.

Hello who's weak now?

My God, My God is so very stronger!

Don't weaken me to the point that you can be strong

ATTACK

I thought about our men who warred for our country. In their methods of training to defend our nation. I was wondering how and when they mapped out the enemy's camp to destroy, if all went as planned to win a never-ending war?

They studied them by social contact. Some even became a socialist. You know the kind that interact. Why?

To learn the method of attack.

One would have to be attacked to know how to attack?

Who lead these attackers to me? Was it them who didn't defend me?

Who can explain to their leaders a cultural illegal mindset of hate and crime? Mistrusting glares staring with formed hate in their minds.

Learned ways of communication. Who let them in my camp? Guards where are you?

Attack!

HEARTLESS PEOPLE DO HEARTLESS THINGS

Excuse me, let's get to the heart of the problem. Who was it again that hurt you? Why are you so mean and angry inside? Was it something I said, I cried? What spirit has you so bitter inside?

No don't pull that trigger. Don't beat me again? I never meant you any harm Sir I was just trying to provide for my family.

Heartless people do heartless things.

Why are you screaming at me? Why do you say such horrible words? That's not that child's name. They did not make you angry. Don't you know your words can build or tear down a person's character?

Heartless people say heartless things.

While waiting in a line at the grocery store she rudely pushed me out of her way. How dare they push me in the back of the line for what? Didn't she see us waiting in line Mommy? People are just rude they are just heartless and they do heartless things.

Why would they say so much hateful words about that person? What good will ever come out of such gossip? Do they want to destroy a land? Do they want to start a war? Why would they twist up her words? Because…heartless people do heartless things?

Why did he spit in that man's face? Why did she murder her children? Why are their eyes filled with so much dark? That smile was wicked, get ready they are ready to attack.

Heartless people do heartless things.

A Desperate Cry For Help!

Have you ever heard someone cry for help? A desperate scream or a silent whisper? Their heart filled with so much pain from years of rejection and shame. A cry for attention and there is no one there to listen. Where does one run in such desperation?

Someone said to go to church. Someone said go to your parents. Someone said go to God in prayer. While being directed I did and what happened? I'm right back where I started. Does anyone see the force of isolation?

They are trying to steal everything that I worked so hard for. My life, my child, my education, my career. Where do I go, who do I turn too? I cannot pray because I am not their kind. I cannot speak because they will use it against me. Did you know because of my belief I'm considered abnormal?

God, can't you hear my cry? I thought you were a God of the present help? You said all I had to do is trust you when I pray and believe. You said you would turn my circumstances around. Who is telling me that you won't answer? Who is challenging me in such unbelief? I trusted you on yesterday. Why don't I have faith today? Can you get me from all these liars, back sliders, cheaters, stealers, murderers, and hear my cry? See my tears? Answer my cry?

You said to make my request known unto you. God, they are trying to kill me. Will you protect me? Will you send your guardian angels or light to direct me out of this dark tunnel? I hear the hearts of people who just don't know you so they want me to be desperate with them. They want me in their shoes. They want me to suffer because why? Do you hear me yet?

I thought you brought me out of this cycle of failure and defeat? I'm tired of taking someone else's pain. It wasn't my war or fight. I'm innocent. He killed himself. They killed others. I was raped of my life because of who? What disposition they are trying to gain? Do you think they will shut up if I take the blame? Do you think the war will be over then?

If I said I was born and that's why all the trouble came on me. Somedays God I wished I just did not exist. I wished that I would not carry the world on my shoulders. I wished that I could get into the minds of others and say get me out of their thoughts and mouth. I wished I had no name to identify me and just be another number. Do you hear me yet? It was not my fault. A desperate cry of no one's lover.

I need your unconditional love. I need your unchanging hand. I need a touch from you God. Do you have time to listen? If you know all and hear all why won't you show up for me? Did I deny you? Did I say that you never existed? Am I the one who is trying to take matters in my hand and stop trying?

I need your help Dear Lord. Please forgive me for being others. Please get me out of this story line, this play, or movie. I don't want to be this star anymore. I'm not even getting paid for all this drama that they call talent.

A desperate cry for help….Hear my cry Oh Lord. I need you in the mist of this storm.

GET RID OF ME SET ME FREE!

Do you ever feel like someone is controlling you? As if you are their Muppet or raggedy Annie.

They are in your mind 24-7. They know your every move. They follow you to torment you. Tell them to go!

Get rid of me set me free. I am no one's slave to be mastered. I am no one's tool to be used. Didn't you know who is the master planner? Micro manage yourself!

Who have be-witched you?

Dear ladies and gentlemen, a letter from the wise. Wait! There are spiritual bondages that come in through relationship building called soul tides. Some hateful women and men would like to have power and rule over you. Sometimes it comes through the dominant women in men's life too and vice versa. I encourage you to always pray before you make a commitment.

Commitments are choices that you make. Some people make them when picking the right school to receive your education. Some people make them when picking the right careers. Some make them in choosing the right mate to build families. They are made to structure your future for their own prosperity and growth.

When making these choices they may or may not be the right choice. The only way you know it's right, there will be confirmation. The statue may look good or book cover may look good on the outside but once you are in it's hard to get out. You could be trapped in a bunch of mess if you don't have boldness or confidence. That's why it's important to pray first.

It's true sometimes you will never know if you don't try. Try to be wise in your choosing because a wrong mate or choice is hard to get rid of. You should never be haunted with regret. You should never be in fear because it will be the right choice.

If you make a mistake in choosing, don't ever beat yourself up or allow those who have be-witched you, to have the upper power. If God is for you who can be against you. Never trust your enemies. Always have a relationship with your Heavenly Father for guidance.

How would you know they are your enemies? They are in your mind to gain and control.

GET RID OF ME AND SET ME FREE!

Get rid of me, you, unlawful spirit, you have no power, control, or rule

Didn't you know I am God's property?

Get rid of me; you old hateful boss, teacher, counselor who never had the patience to see what I am truly worth. I thought you cared.

Get rid of me my once friend

Get out of my mind so that I can be free!

Free yourself from your controls that once structured me.

Get rid of me! You old hateful devil using my face for mockery.

Get rid of me! You old witch you have no power here!

Hey Jezy is that you controlling the city, the town, the church, who is your rule?

What is your purpose that you are trying to prove?

Honey never let them rule!

Never fall in the trap of failure

Let failure build you too! It is all in your hand to rule.

God take control over our country. God take control over our nation. God take control over our families. God take control over our cities, our jobs, and our schools.

Satan let me go! So that I can be free!

Get rid of me so God can rule!

Get me out of your circle of haters!

In your minds get rid of me, my once friend you know who you are,

Scratch me out of your sight, blacken my name, cross me off of your list too!

So that we can all be free!

I Am Not Your Punching Bag I Am Not Your Excuse!

Have you ever seen a mad woman or man going around grumbling, fussing, and cussing at everyone because of whatever? They are fidgety, they can't be still, and if spoken to wrongly they snap with their dukes up ready to fight. Before you know it there's a punching match going. Honey, you were their excuse to release whatever it is from them, not getting help.

I'm not your punching bag or excuse for whatever harmed you. Please put down your fists. Stop balling them up to swing at me. Was I really the one who made you mad today? Did you get out on the wrong side of the bed? I am not your excuse for what made you mad. Please leave your problems at the door.

I am not your punching bag or excuse for whatever has driven your emotions of envy and jealousy. Why are you fighting me? Was it really something I said? I saw your wondering eyes from day one. I saw how you stared at me, watching my every move, listening to everything I said. Can we tell the truth; I am not your excuse. Please get some help.

Shrugging your shoulders turning your nose up. Your face turned red. Hello, is there something you need to get out? I am not your excuse to vandalize, terrorize, or scrutinize my name. Is there something you're trying to hide? Let the truth be told, this war is not mine.

Put down your fists and let me help you out. I am not your excuse Let's go together and get a punching bag. Let's take the anger out on it and not each other.

I am not your excuse, let's talk about this matter. Why are you threatened? Are you losing your power to control every given matter? Violence is not you. Do you know whose ground you are camping on? Let's fight this crime together.

I am not your excuse or punching bag to fight off your pain. Let us reason with one another. I know you are having relationship problems. Your children are probably driving you bonkers. I know that you are having problems in your home and on your job. You are probably very uncertain, but I refuse to be your punching bag or excuse.

Can't you see this battle is not mine or yours; this battle is the Lords. I'm tired of hearing your yells. I'm tired of your cursing. I know you're having a bad day but let me escape it. Let's turn it into a good one. Come on close your eyes and let's count to 10. Can you walk away and breathe? Better yet, let's go take a walk and get a breath of fresh air? I am and will never be your excuse to bully me or tame me into you. Don't you know who my master is? Michael the warring angel is released on my behalf. Touch not the anointed and do his prophet no harm. Take your dukes and fight no more.

I am not your punching bag or your excuse!

BEAT HER MASTER IT WASN'T ME!

Today I was thinking about the handmaidens in the bible who were made servants to the masters. You read about them in the bible. They were the ones who were used by the Kings and Queens to bare children, to clean, to work, to feed, and etc. When they were out of line, they were beaten with 50 lashes.

I thought of the fair skinned girl who was pointed out by the dark-skinned girl who told the masters to beat her to cover up her own shame. She said, uh-hah it was her, beat her master it wasn't me. She ratted out the other for her own selfish gain. What did she want? More money or power to rule?

There are histories telling the hidden truth of this type of abuse. I was a slave to both white and dark people sins. I was a slave to their many whips. Always being chastised, rebuked, and scorned. I was the blame for unlawful behaviors. Beaten down with words and other people's pain.

I may have been a prodigy of my master's disgrace. When will this type of crime stop? Will it ever end? I was the little girl beaten for no apparent reason. I hear it like yesterday, her cries saying Master no Master No it wasn't me. Beat her Master it wasn't me.

This is how I know the truth on race, on race crimes, religious ungodly behaviors, corporate punishments and hazing of others still exist. There are people still being hung on a tree due to the orders of their master.

Master Jesus, protect me from these dead spirits that are trying to be risen. Free me from the KKK, white supremacy, and unholy organizations.

Protect my family if they come after me to beat me. They're trying to burn me. Help me escape from their slaying. Free me Master do not let them beat me anymore. It was not me!

SET MY PEOPLE FREE!

¹³ Then the LORD said to Moses, "Get up early in the morning, confront Pharaoh and say to him, 'This is what the LORD, the God of the Hebrews, says: Let my people go, so that they may worship me,

Exodus, 9-13, NIV

Have you ever been in bondage? Enslaved to other people, enslaved to sin? This is the most horrible place to be. Always harkening to someone else's commands. Getting beat in the back for not obeying the master of the whip. Are you like the children of Israel under a lordship or king who has no heart?

God wants you free!

Have you ever been encaptivated in your mind? Listening to Satan's commands. Obeying the words of his defeat? Not knowing God's words through Jesus Christ and you always fall into his traps through wandering thoughts that do not glorify the Lord your God?

God wants you free!

Have you ever been in a place where free worship is not known, heard of, or done? Hearkening to the demands of your authorities. Being moved on the emotions of those who are before you. Not truly free to be happy, free to love people and the Lord your God?

God truly wants you free!

Have you ever been lured to other spirits through emotions or their communications? Where certain words through manipulation draws you in and they try to befriend you to stab you in the back or toss you to the dogs?

God wants you free!

Free from ungodly persuasions, free from demons and free from lusts. Free from promiscuous behaviors. Free from street gang violence. Free from unlawful politics. Free from street drugs. Free from horrible habits. Free from your enemies. Free from Satan's allurements of gossip. Free from unknown visitors in your mind. Free from invaders that tell you to shut-up and bow to their commands.

Whom the Son of God sets free is free indeed!

This is what I declare and decree on this day and very hour, you are free.

Free from sin if you like?

Free from those Warlocks, if you like?

Free from the demons, if you like?

Free to be happy. Free to be saved. Free from underground authority, if you like?

Free from dark languages and communications of cursing.

Free from the curse.

Free from being a slave to your enemies.

Free from death threats and mind games from Satan's authority.

Free from dark unreligious rules.

Free from cigarettes. Free from drugs. Free from alcohol. Free from addictions. Free from every small god in your life that does not magnify the Almighty God.

Satan has no rule; he is trampling on God's property.

God says go. Set my people free!

Just as Moses obeyed God's command, I declare you Satan to go! Set God's People FREE! This is what the Lord, the God of the Hebrews, says: "Let my people go!"

If you believe in the Son of God, allow him to take over all of your mind, heart, fears, and emotions by confessing with your mouth and believing in your heart. He will free you.

Let God lead you through Jesus Christ and the Holy Spirit out of bondage!

DON'T!

Don't back me in a corner so that you can shine!

Don't muffle me so that you can get rich off my thought or dreams.

Don't put me in the back of the line so you can snatch what's rightfully mine.

Building off my dreams, desires, and everything that I waited so long for…

MY SUCCESS!

Don't shut me up so your lies can destroy my world

Do you know who you are messing with?

Destroying my character

There's a law now

Are you ready to pay for my success?

Who started this crime anyways?

Was it I?

I don't think so….

Don't you get it

Black on Black, white supremacy, nation against nation or what is it called?

Are we in the perilous times?

I'm gonna get mine!

Not by slander you're NOT!!

Don't back me in the corner for your lies, hate, and deceit.

Didn't you know that I had dreams!

That was definitely for me.

Watch me succeed.

Get out of my way so that I can fly!

Stop blocking my view

Because it was never about you or I

Didn't you know God gave me a brain too?

Don't twist my words up so you can have a treaty against me.

Who started this BOYCOTT anyways? Don't you see my picketing signs?

This is not the Boston Tea Party!

In God's kingdom, there's one goal in mind.

I will get everything I deserve.

So, will God, all in return.

He said vengeance is mine…

It's war time

Can't you hear my war cry?

DON'T!

It's Not A Figment of Our Imagination

It's not a figment of our imagination

That the curse of racial profiling continues to grow from the 19th throughout the 20th and 21st Century

The number of blacks being pulled over by policemen. Reading headlines of those being beat brutally tormented by the ones we trust… When will it stop?

Plots to stop prosperity and growth for another black person who you feel is already blessed.

That your face turns red in anger and mind imagines more hate and murder. Is it jealousy

That your formed social groups and polls to discriminate against a person once like you.

It's not a figment of our imagination

That you fell into your enemy's plan to divide and strife for whomever mastered you.

It's not a figment of our imagination

That you came into our camp to learn us and to start a war in our minds. Is it so you can distract us from whatever you're trying to gain?

Get Out!!

Hello, don't you know that I hear you and God's eyes are watching you?

That was a low blow!

It's not a figment of our imagination

In your mind you already labeled me, placed me in many categories of people that does not even describe me.

Didn't you know you were a part of their study too?

Hi, my name is…Let me tell you about a man named Jesus

It's not a figment of our imagination!

I'm Ready

When I'm healed from brokenness

When I'm delivered from past hurts

When chains of darkness are broken

When generations before me are organized, and restored

I'm ready to give you all that I am

When your heart is restored

When you're healed from all brokenness and

Chains of bondages have fallen

Baby I'll be all yours

I'm ready you ready?

Let's together be restored!

LET ME INTRODUCE YOU TO MY COUNSELOR

Let me introduce you to my counselor

His name is all that I need

He came to me just as I was

He showed me something very precious

His love

My best friend

Very wise he is

Special and dear

He revealed knowledge that I never knew

He found ways for me to submit, so that I could obey and listen

He made things very understandable

He counseled me in ways no one could

Do you know him?

Let me give you his number 1-800- JESUS

My interpreter

My Counselor

My Savior

How sweet is he?

Very!

Proverbs 31 Woman is who I am

I thought you knew!

Let me introduce you to my counselor!

All My Life I Had To Fight!

All my life I had to fight. I didn't want to but it was forced by who?

I had to fight for righteous standards.

I had to fight for my position in life.

I had to fight for my freedom.

I had to fight for my God given rights.

I had to fight for my education.

Why?

Was it for you?

I had to fight because somehow, I couldn't belong.

Was it because of you?

This is my area, this is my room, these are my things, that is mine and not yours.

This is my career

I chose this place and position and why?

Was it because of my color, my beliefs, my dreams or theirs?

Why fight me? You are the one that's looking stupid here.

All my life I had to fight

To stay focused and aim for the prize.

Why are they attacking me now? Why are they trying to blame me? For what?

My God changed my destiny

I've changed my destiny for you honey. Can't you see?

No longer a statistic

If they attack me I did it for you to see

Racial, religious, and gender discrimination

Horrible politics to ruin my family's name

You don't have to let them pull you into their mess

Fighting for what's right you'll never go wrong

Let him fight for you!

You belong!

All my life I had to fight. What's really wrong?

DREAMS AND VISIONS

A Star For The Day

If you were to give yourself a star, what would it be for? When we were in kindergarten a star was given for good behavior, for a good grade, or a good deed you've done for that week.

How did you feel? Was it a big accomplishment? Was it something that you couldn't wait to go home and tell your parents and family members about?

Running through the door putting it on the table and waiting to get your reward or sometimes just getting a pat on the back, or a big hug and words of encouragement like, "Keep up the good work. Better yet, do you remember your parents saying, "Let's make a deal, if you get two more there will be a monetary reward, clothes, or gift?

Wouldn't it be great to think about the reward given from heaven?

The biggest star ever given

The rewards on earth are out numbered

When you think about all the accomplishments on earth, they could be nothing compared to the Great rewards in heaven.

The many many stars in the sky are unnumbered. Wish for it. They belong to you, grab it, it's yours.

Being blessed on earth would be one great goal for anyone who believes

It is only gained through perseverance and persistence

Just as that little girl or boy it's something to work hard for.

Do you have a star for the day?

Blessed are they that are meek; for they shall inherit the earth. Matthew 5:5

IN MY EYES

In my eyes, I see diamonds that sparkle so bright a five-caret ring broken in three because of the promises it will bring

In my eyes, I see many little princesses and kings climbing to the top of their mountains reaching to the top of their dreams.

In my eyes, I see giants falling getting out of the way so that I can accomplish my dreams.

In my eyes, I see people falling and kneeling to the feet of Jesus, so humbled to accomplish these things.

In my eyes, I see a love so great that cannot be stigmatized.

In my eyes, there's many trees as people fulfilling the same dreams that you described.

In my eyes, I see hearts in the color of gold that fills the room with laughter and the abundance that only God brings.

In my eyes, I see people embracing each other with love and telling stories of every accomplishment that God allowed them to achieve.

In my eyes, I see the favor of God because of my agape love and human nature that only He brings.

In my eyes, I see smiles of gladness due to the wonderful songs of joy that lifts every heart to righteousness.

In my eyes, I'll always see the little girl that you are who matured to the young lady that you will always be.

In my eyes, I see that beautiful white dress and trails of length for that handsome young man that we know will bring you fruit of gladness because your self-worth will always come unmatched.

In my eyes I see a lot, no one can steal, to what I can only imagine

Because in my eyes there are no lies it tells it all

It covers all with the love of Christ and never releases those hidden things.

In my eyes, there are mysteries being unfolded but, only tears of joy that allow me to embrace everything

In my eyes, no one could ever imagine

Only in my eyes will you see God's favor unfolded rains of promises that only He told…

HEAVEN ON EARTH

But God, who is rich in mercy, for his great love wherewith he loved us, even when we were dead in sins, hath quickened us together with Christ, (by grace ye are saved;) And hath raised [us] up together, and made [us] sit together in heavenly [places] in Christ Jesus: Ephesians 2:4-6, KJV

Last night I dreamed that you came to earth to help me with some of my troubles. I wanted so badly for others to see You how I did. I wanted them to feel your presence, and to come into the knowledge of knowing that You are so real.

The murdering and wars of innocent lives shed. Little black boys and girls murdered for no reason is that enough to be said? The loud cries of their mother's heart, is what I heard or was it theirs as they landed to your hands.

You came down and shined your light with such white and heavenly glow. I wanted so badly to pay back these men for their wrongful killings. There were so many shattered hopes and dreams snatched because of one man's pride. You see God, I know it must be Jesus to bring me to a place of peace and erase my thoughts of sins.

You ascended on high it was just as I imagined. While others were warring, and caught up in all the madness you allowed me to see and experience You in your presence.

It was like wings that held me in the air while You were going up to sit with God in the heavenly places. I now know it was your white robe that glowed so bright. I really couldn't see if you had them in your hands but, I knew I didn't have to fear because I was at a still in your presence.

I stood still and such amazement and awe. I reached my arms like a child asking to go with you. In my heart, I know that it was really you.

As I woke up, the atmosphere was so peaceful. Is it heaven on earth that I am experiencing? I feel your presence is so near and dear. This place of stillness, quietness, and serene, I know your presence is so real. Filling my heart with such joy when it seems like everything else is falling apart, it can only be you Jesus to let me get a glimpse of heaven.

I know you heard my prayers for peace, because you wouldn't allow me to experience it. To be seated with you and know that you are yet on the throne no more worries, no more fears, no more tears, because I know you're there.

You reminded me of my prayers. I cried, "God…Jesus are you there? Do you see what's going on down here on earth? Can you hear and see what I do? Please protect my family and friends from all hurt, harm and danger." You responded in a dream to let me know that they were all in your hands.

Thank you, God, for answering my prayers and quieting the chaos of darkness and letting me sit in heavenly places in Christ Jesus. Thank you for shinning your grace down on me and allowing me to experience your kindness through Christ Jesus. Thank you for allowing me to experience you and know you in your glory. The peace that only you give that you reign down from the heavens.

The joy that only you allow us to experience on earth in your glory it's Heaven on earth.

In the last couple of years, I have seen one headline after another of news of innocent lives shed because of power and greed. If one over steps their boundary or show any disrespect to a culture, then one will have to pay. It's sad to say that evil principalities and rulers of darkness, are trying to destroy our land.

The Bible says that God's people will be protected from this type of evilness throughout the land which, leads me to a better understanding on how they will be protected. It is only in the sacred relationship and knowing him in the beauty of His holiness. Through prayer and time spent with God, He will give one power to fight against the enemies who are defeated at the root.

The question comes to mind, "What about the martyrs?" Martyrs are Christians who are taking a stand for Christ. They are the people who are being beheaded by the ISIS savages. The physical attacks of the innocent, has to stop in Jesus Name! I believe that God will put an end to all confusion and the innocent will be protected.

The physical attacks and the mental attacks through hate crimes such as racism has been silent but at the same time, loud for years. The cries are finally being heard and it's sad to say, they are being heard after the crime is done. It will only take the power of people through love that will destroy the plot of the enemy's plan.

I believe that the people will be protected through the power of love and that is only through Jesus Christ. It's the only way! The respect for human life through God's expectation will be the only way to bring order throughout the land. Power should only come from above and rule. There should be respect for human rights no matter what color, race, religion, or creed. Morality can come through a Unitarian approach. The society that you live in should have temperance, order, and justification where sin will not be magnified but, destroyed.

I will always look to Jesus who is the author and finisher of my faith. I have greater faith to believe that even my children's children will be set free from the snare of the enemy. This will come through faith and obedient sacrifice; most of all through the power of prayer. I believe that united we stand and divided we fall. The leaders are being made to lead and not destroy the hope and faith of the innocent lives around them. It will take Christian Leaders who know how to be led by God's power and not to fall in the traps of Satan's plan for destruction that drives on division, strife, jealousy, envy, murdering, etc.

I'M A GO GETTER, NOT A GOLD DIGGER

I'm a go getter when I have dreams and accomplish them.

I'm a go getter when all odds are against me and I have nothing but faith to carry me through.

I'm a go getter not a gold digger.

I'm a go getter when it seems like I'm all alone climbing the mountains that are placed on my path to success. Not taking the short cuts or asking someone to find me another way, but speaking to that mountain telling it to get of my way.

I'm a go getter and not a gold digger. Achieving, striving, and progressing to my destiny. Not stumbling or falling at the traps of my enemies' hands.

When the signs for success is pursued and not hidden or snatched. I'm a go getter and not a gold digger.

When my future is not centered around a man or woman, a boy or girl to dig me out of my hurts, burdens, or bondages because I have favor that's not connected to gender or things, but is given by my Heavenly Father above, through my obedience and sacrifice.

I'm a go getter and not a gold digger. When I can say, "My hard work has paid off every challenge of distress, because, it was not my trust in man but, my trust in God that got me down life's highways of success.

Gold Digger where you at? It's not about I, It's not about you….

Follow God's plans for success. Dig to please your heavenly Father. Follow His plans, He has it all for you on this righteous path.

Go getter, flaunt your stuff. No more giving up! Rise and shine because hard work pays off.

Never hold your hand out! Just be rewarded, for great is His faithfulness and great is His love.

I'm a winner not a gold digger!

My Desire

Lord you said that you know the plans that you have for me and that is to prosper as my soul prosper and be in good health, wealth, and peace of mind.

You said in your word that if I keep my mind stayed on thee thy will keep me in perfect peace.

You are not the author of confusion, Satan called Lucifer is. He was rejected by God because he wanted to be God. He wanted to have all of his glory. So, he was sent to hell.

My desire is that God the Father be ruler over my thoughts, my heart, my mind, and my temple. For you know the plans you have for me. You know my dreams. You know the desires of my heart.

Help me and everyone to believe in your Word. Help those who don't understand to understand, if they desire. If not, allow us that understand to experience the peace that you promised.

The power through receiving the Holy Spirit so that we know that you know our desire

My desire is your desire in Jesus' Name.

Lord let thy will be done!

A Man That Can Praise God Is A Keeper

That I may shew forth all thy praise in the gates of the daughter of Zion: I will rejoice in thy salvation. Psalms 9:14, KJV

The day I heard the cry of the voice of triumph, a warrior, a man of praise is what God revealed to me. Your leap of faith proved your strength and courage.

No one knew but God, why your praise was so loud.

Signs of joy and laughter never proud.

The humble cry, the warriors sound gave my heart pleasure to see such a man with great holy stature.

Was this one who spoke to his mountains?

A man, a holy man that can praise God is a keeper!

But thou art holy; Oh, God inhabits the praises of his people, his men,

that are not too ashamed of what man may think.

Was he looking or feeling for a beat to dance to the tunes of the organ and drum that speaks?

No! Not at all his praise moved the room; it broke the atmosphere of fear, shame, doubt and defeat…

This man, a holy man's leap of faith held back nothing on this day.

His fight of faith showed me this is

a man of honor who proved his father's praise with his feet in every step forward.

The power and the anointing on that day released heaven to reveal that a man who can praise my God is a keeper!

The bible says the anointing destroys all yokes.

This man is a preacher man did I say.

No hidden pride or anything he was trying to prove, I don't believe.

This man, a whole man,

A complete man;

A prudent man, who was tried and tested in his faith but conquered everything that was trying to hold him bound, took charge of Satan's defeat and praised his God.

He's a keeper!

When praises go up blessings come down were signs of truth in this man's feet.

God's glory rained down blessings in every word this man spoke.

God revealed his lifestyle of holiness, righteousness, set apart from darkness.

A man that can praise God is a keeper

Signs of freedom, signs of justice, and signs of love to the same Father God I know.

Um-Um-Um

This man who praised God, I know is a keeper

Is he for me?

Is he all that God kept for me?

Is he the one God told me to wait for?

Were the questions in my mind? While praising God on that day, he revealed to me there is power behind his praise!

Later God revealed, that it was heaven who answered each cry in his praise.

A man, a holy man, a righteous man, who praises God, is a keeper!

EMBRACE ME AGAIN

The other day I remembered your touch that made me tremble. It was so gentle. I could never imagine something so real. There is no one like you. Will you embrace me again?

You wiped every tear from my eyes, you took away every guilt, stain, and shame.

You made me to believe that you were so real and dear Lord

Will you embrace me again?

Where are you? Are you there? I haven't felt your touch in a while? Are you there? Will you embrace me again?

Have I done anything to run you away?

You told me that you will never leave me nor forsake me

Let me kneel and pray

I need you in my life. Please don't leave me now?

Let me see, feel your touch, show me a sign that you are near…

If I apologize, for every thought that was not pleasing, will you remove the dark cloud so that I can see you and feel you?

Is there anything that I am harvesting in my heart that is not giving you the satisfaction and glory you deserve….am I grieving you?

Will you embrace me again?

My father's touch will wipe away all my pain. You said it!

Please don't leave me

I will get rid of everything that's distracting me so that I can feel your touch again.

I can't be alone now.

If I pray your Word? Stay in your Word? Believe in your Word? Sacrifice a meal a day?

Make a vowel to you and never let it go?

Will you embrace me again?

Who came in between us?

Was it my thoughts?

Was it my pride?

Was it my inpatient way of thinking?

Will you remove these stones of emptiness? Come into my heart again Jesus? Can you hear me? I need you to embrace me in your arms again.

There's freedom there, love there, peace there, joy there, and most of all there's strength there….

Embrace me my King? Perfect me in your warm embrace.

Embrace me in your arms again.

If we confess our sins, he is faithful and just to forgive us our sins, and to cleanse us from all unrighteousness. If we say that we have not sinned, we make him a liar, and his word is not in us. I John 1:9-10, KJV

THE PERFECT ME

Be ye therefore perfect, as your Heavenly Father is perfect. (Matt. 5:48, KJV)

Who is perfect and what perfects us? This is the question that comes to several people's mind, especially when all imperfections are seen. Imperfections of life challenges of shame, hurt, and defeat. Who needs them? Not I!

The perfect me will tell the imperfections to get out the way of God's purposed. To let them know they have no place on God's ground. His solid sure foundation and His promises.

The perfect me would press through life struggles and come out on top of the world with life's gains through patience. It would let the perfect shine through alleys and valleys of darkness.

The perfect me, would love unconditionally until the imperfections are gone. Never comparing to the other because the perfect knows what perfect is all about.

The perfect me is redeemed, set a part in God's glory, travailing and praising him for the perfect accomplished never ashamed and victorious. Me!

The perfect me would: gain, achieve, strive, and succeed through obedience and righteous living; staying very humble and Godly proud to boast on His accomplishments and not mine.

If it had not been for the Lord on my side where would I be?

The perfect I (me)… will only allow Christ to be glorified so excellence can be magnified. I would never be anyone else's imperfections because I am perfect can't you see?

The Dew In The Morning Rest Fresh Upon My Heart

The morning dew is the light film that is seen on people's decks and the grass. It's the white on the leaves and tree branches. It shines so bright. It's a fresh smell of rain. When the sun shines upon it, it reminds me of fresh new glory.

My heart is at peace to know that God has showered his love and presence through the natural beauty that He only gives.

It's a wonderful sight and it's a message from the heavens letting us know that His glory is resting upon the earth. Not only upon the earth, but upon our hearts, to whom that believes and trusts in His amazing love.

The morning dew is God's glory! Trust in His power to shine through our hearts for joy, peace, and love. Just like the son that shines with the rain, the sparkle will never go away. Because it's God's love through Jesus Christ that will forever shine. A spiritual and natural glow that will never dim, if you stay in His presence.

Welcome dew in the morning.

Jesus rest upon us all!

The dew in the morning stay fresh upon our hearts!

CAN'T NOBODY STEAL MY DREAM!

"Our lives begin to end the day we become silent about things that matter."

— Martin Luther King Jr., I Have a Dream: Writings and Speeches That Changed the World

This writing was inspired by a 10-year-old little girl whose heart was crying for change to happen in her and her family's life. – A.E.

I sat down with a little girl whose heart was crying out for change in her family's poverty situation. She asked me to pray for her and her family. I asked, "What is it specifically that she wanted to pray for?" She said I want religion in my life. I said do you want Jesus in your life and she said, "Yes."

I asked, "Is that it?" Is there anything else you would like to request from God? Because, he is the God of the impossible and he can do anything if you believe. He wants to bless you. She then opened with very specific things I dare not mention because it was between me, her, and God.

A little girl whose bed was the floor that she shares with three other families. She knew of no bed and who never really had order or discipline in her life, heart cried out on that evening as we prayed. I then asked her to write down everything she desires from God and she did.

That morning before she left she looked at me with tears running from her eyes saying, "Can't Nobody Steal My Dream!" I said," No they can't!" I told her to dream aloud. Study real hard and never stop praying because God hears her prayers!

Have you ever had a moment where you wanted to help change the lives of the innocent? In your mind you're thinking, "That you will do almost anything out of desperation for them to have a better life?" How can one lead them in the right direction? When…

Some people complain about the most stupid things. Their eyes should be opened to appreciate everything. Yet, they still complain.

I wanted so badly to take this young girl under my wings. Her sister and brother too, but they didn't want to leave their dad.

I cried to God, for his help. The same God that did it for me will be the same God to set this little girl free! He is no respecter of person.

" Then Peter opened his mouth, and said, Of a truth I perceive that God is no respecter of persons: But in every nation he that feareth him, and worketh righteousness, is accepted with him." Acts 10:34-35

This little girl reminded me of myself. What an amazing God I serve! He humbles us that in that way. Doesn't he?

CAN'T NOBODY STEAL MY DREAM!

I dream that I will one day have a house for my family.

I dream that one day my father will be stable enough to lead his family.

I love my daddy! He's just sad. I wish he could get a job so that we can be happy.

I dream that I will become a doctor, nurse, or hair stylist.

I dream that my family's love for one another will never die.

Can't nobody steal my dream!

I dream that one day my sisters and brothers will see that I am smart.

I dream that I will have the same favor of God that brought them out.

I dream that everyone who tried to stop my dream will see that ...

Can't nobody steal my dream!

I dream that when God grants me my dream that I will not repeat every bad thing.

I dream that when I grow up that my children will be set free.

I dream that I can experience life to the fullest and my family will see me free.

Can't nobody steal my dream!

I dream that I can one day travel the world and see every momentum spot

I dream that my president, "An African American Male" face will be placed on Mt. Rushmore.

Can't nobody steal my dream!

I dream that when I sit down to study, that my life's circumstances will never make me stop.

I dream that I can stay focused until I reach the very top!

Can't nobody steal my dream!

Inspired and co-written by a 10 year old little girl named, Alexcys.

IF YOU DON'T LIVE FOR WHAT YOU BELIEVE ...

"Then What Are You Living For? I am A Woman Hear Me Roar!" (Helen Reddy)

I believe that life is what you make it to be. If there are pathways given for a road of success and you don't know how to go down that road do you get off, because of traps of distractions? Who mislead you not to believe in you?

Who muted you to a life of oppression? Was it you? Do you know your purpose? If you don't live for what you believe in, then what are you living for?

Do you live for those who betrayed you, confused you, and labeled you? Do you live for others who said you will never achieve or amount to anything? Do you live for those who abandoned you and scrutinized the character of your very being?

I understood the feminist cry for freedom and a purpose in a manmade society whose strength is gained from woman. No longer, will I hide what God has created me to be....

Unique, intelligent, gifted woman with heart full of love. I am compassionate, empathetic, a leader who hears the cry of other children, women and men. Never mute me, degrade me or hide my talents I am a woman hear me roar!

One who knows her own quality and never has to accept anything less than what God has purposed! One who turns heads with strides gained from hard work, unseen sweat, and overcome challenges.

I believe in me, I am a woman, I choose a life full of abundance, I gain success through overcoming my knockdowns; I know I have a purpose to conquer. I am a woman: bold, beautiful, woman, who has a word to heal the sick, raise the dead (both natural and spiritual), who striving, conquering, never giving up.....Here me roar!

KEEP ME AND LET ME FLY!

Keep me and let me fly with you to places unheard. Let's explore everything that love brings. Let's explore the most wonderful hidden things.

Keep me and let's color the earth with God's wonderful love.

Keep me so that we can both be creative. Can I show you the truth?

My talents are hidden and made to be seen.

Keep me so that we can build together. Let us never wonder.

Keep me and Let's fly to the moon and back watching star lights to brighten and sparkle in our eyes.

Keep me and Let's together go to the streets pulling those off, healing people's wounds.

Let's together imagine what our God can do.

Keep me so we can together achieve great things and dream.

Can't you imagine,

Implementing the plans for growing people and not allowing them to be instruments for destruction?

Keep me and let me fly.

I know I am worth it and you will never regret your choice.

Keep me and let me fly.

I Want My Own Island

I want my own island where I would be able to live a life of privacy and peace.

Where the only people that enter in will have access through only me.

A place of quietness.

A place of relaxation.

A place of me being complete.

I want my own island.

Where I can build a family and structure it to love the traditions that I teach (which has so much meaning and purpose).

A place to rekindle the fire that was blown out.

A place to reign.

I want my own island.

Where the birds wake us up at the crack of dawn and the water hitting against the ocean shore.

I want my own island.

Smelling the tropical flowers seeing the deep blue colors.

I want my own island.

Dancing to the serenaded songs that you wrote.

I want my own island keeping everyone out, a place of being happy about life, caring about nothing.

I want my own island to relax and shoot the breeze under the sun sipping on non-alcoholic fruit drinks.

I want my own island where famous people go to run, full of security leaving all paparazzi behind.

I want my own island.

Let's together run and find it.

Where the only people can enter have their own yachts and fun.

HIDE MY EMOTIONS SO THAT I CAN SEE

Sometimes I feel like screaming aloud when I don't know what direction I am going.

When I'm distracted and when my plans are held up by the unknown. Things begin to get cloudy and I cannot see what direction I am going.

This is when I get very angry and want to scream but I usually begin to cry aloud…Lord, hide my emotions so that I can see where you're leading me.

How about when others, out of ignorance, can't hear me when I speak and they say I don't understand you, when you are speaking clear English.

Lord hide my emotions so that I can see through other people's pride.

Lord, hide my emotions so that I can see.

What you are doing when everything seems chaotic,

Family is out of control,

Relationships

Health

Tormented by fear

Lord hide my emotions

From these lies…

God help me hear what others are hearing?

Help me see what others are seeing or hide me from such disgrace.

Sometimes I wish I knew sign language and where others can communicate my language.

Where just a look or sign would acknowledge, who dwells within my heart.

Lord hide my emotions. So, that when I worship, people don't misinterpret my gratitude and love as depression.

Sometimes I feel like screaming, when I see others in need and mistreated.

Lord hide my emotions. So, that I can see what it is that you are doing and hear what you are saying...

YOU HAVE THE POWER TO CHANGE YOUR STORY...

Everyone has a story that made them to be who they are today. Stories of hardship and how they made it over to easy street. Stories of sadness that sometimes took too long to heal. Stories of brokenness that made them grow and mature.

Most of us escaped life threatening situations and were able to turn their life around. Some never knew hardship and was born with a silver spoon. No matter what destination of defeat you are heading, you have power to change your story.

Dark areas that are so vague just passing through life not knowing your way, you too have the power to change your story!

Living in the ghetto never coming out of poverty, cultivated lifestyles with no promise. Did you know that you too have a story and have power to change it? Yes, you!

Living out your parents' story never knowing your own because, they were trying to find their own. Helping others find their way down a journey of success and not knowing how to conquer your own. Avenues of misleading directions shared moments of time wasted? Hello you...Yea you! You have the power to change your story.

Careers of learning, never knowing if life really matters. What is your destination, where are you going? Time is money and money is time. Isn't it grace that we all need to gain this authority? Hey, you! Can you hear me now? You have the power to change your story.

Power is in your hands. Power is in your words. Power comes from above: to walk right, talk right, and yes, sometimes it takes us just listening to our hearts. You, young lady! You, young man! Have the power to change your story.

I see trees like giants. I see wings as eagles. I see many people like you and me. I see that you have proven your worth through humble strides toward your prize. Fulfilling a childhood dream that God revealed through the night. Hush now, can you hear? Wasn't it you, that said, that one day you were going to be a millionaire?

Yes, that drug dealer that escape a world of defeat, who almost gave up and gave in. Yes, the one who was driven to their wits end. It was you; whose story had no perspective end. Not you?

Yes, that person who almost gave up on life in a suicidal state of mind. Yes, it was you that had others talking and heads turning saying, "Who was it that changed her? You too have the power to change your story.

Almost losing your mind over what? It, he, she, and they were not even worth it. You, my dear, have the power to change your story.

Living in the streets, getting run down, torn down, and God knows what else? You too have the power to change your story.

Come out of darkness Can't you see the light? No more torments but doors opened, for your God given talent from birth.

When I grow up I'm going to be a……. You too have time to dream and live out the promises of God. Every journey can lead you to your success, if you have the mind to believe in you. You my dear, have the power to change your story.

I want to be like me, that woman I dreamed to be. I can! I will change my story to complete this life's journey,

To share to my children's children that there was never a defeated soul but a tomorrow for growth. You too, have a story. A powerful story that didn't happen until Christ came in, to set you free. I'm sorry it wasn't luck; it was God's love. Go and tell someone else that they have the power to change their story!

Hello friend, you too have the power to change your story.

Never blame another for your failures. Always pick yourself up and keep striving because his grace is sufficient, enough for you too!

Who was it that turned your life around? Was it you or God's grace? What was it that open the door of opportunity or closed door that built you and created you to turn another direction? Was it that boss or your neighbor? Who or what empowered you to change your story?

BATTLEFIELD OF THE MIND

My dear child, in life you will feel like the world is caving in and there is no end to the sorrows and pain. That's when you should tap into God's Word and start confessing His Word over your life. Believe it and receive it, then watch things happen for you. Never doubt and pray. Believe things will change.

Nowhere in the Bible does God say you are a failure, mistake, life's excuse for disgrace. This is the enemy's trap to destroy your mind. Speak those things that were not as though they are. There's power in your words. Remember God said it.

When your enemies come up against you, because they did it to the generation before you, confess God's word, that no weapon formed against you will prosper.

My child, you are not a repeated disgrace or failure. You have purpose. You have a promised future. How do I know? Because God's Word says it.

Isn't it amazing that He loved us so much that He gave us his promised word?

Keep your mind stayed on His promises,

always pray His Word,

Know it's you He is talking to in his Word

Remember the perfect peace he promises.

Even, the hidden things

and know how to battle for it!

WHAT DO YOU DO WHEN...

What do you do when you are told you have too much pride?

What do you do when you try to fight against the statistics and become the statistic, because of someone else's insecurities, offenses and hate.

Trying to overcome poverty.

Fighting against "They"?

Some people fight back by dreaming aloud to conquer their American Dream through education and careers.

If it takes a mother and wife to work three jobs and go back to school, so be it. If it takes a father to work long and hard hours for his family's dream and success, so be it.

This is a learned process. Everything does not come easy. Sometimes it's harder to reach your goals than other's but still stride. I was taught by my Grandfather a builder of men, structuring others to stay humble, his example and teachings taught, "You have to work hard to get to the top." I was taught by my Grandmother to never hold your head down, "Hold your head up." I was taught by my mother on how to Dream.

What is the "Poverty Line" anyway? "According to the 2011 US Census Bureau, it is a family of 4 (2 adults, 2 children under 18) that earns less than $23,021.

More than 30 million children are growing up in poverty. In one low income community, there was only one book for every 300 children.

In 2011, nearly 46.2 million Americans were living in poverty.

40% of children living in poverty line are 1.3 times more likely to have developmental delays or learning disabilities than those that do not live in poverty.

By the end of the 4th grade, African-American, Hispanic and low-income students are already 2 years behind grade level. By the time they reach the 12th grade, they are 4 years behind.

In 2013, the drop-out rate for students in the nation was at 8% for African-American youth, 75 for Hispanic youth, and 4% for Asian youth, which are all higher than the drop-out rate for Caucasian youth (4%).

Less than 30% of students in the bottom quarter of incomes enroll in a 4-year school. Among that group – less than 50% graduate."

Yet, we have taken prayer out of our schools and disgraced biblical concepts that formed our Nation through compromise. How can one make it in America? Who is an American striving to live an American Dream? Was America too prideful? How can someone from another country humble me so in this way? I was born to be an American. I was born out of darkness to become a Christian. Is it pride? So be it! I need to have confidence not only in me, my family, but my God! So be it!

Confidence vs. Pride... (Webster Dictionary)

Confidence: the feeling or belief that one can rely on someone or something; firm trust; the state of feeling certain about the truth of something; a feeling of self-assurance arising from one's appreciation of one's own abilities or qualities.

Synonyms: trust, belief, faith, credence, conviction...

Pride: Is an inwardly directed emotion that carries two antithetical meanings with a negative connotation. Pride refers to a foolishly and irrationally corrupt sense of one's personal value, status or accomplishments, used synonymously with hubris. With a positive connotation, pride refers to a humble and a content sense of attachment toward one's own choices and actions, or toward a whole group of people and is a product of praise, independent self-reflection and a fulfilled feeling of belonging.

Philosophers and social psychologists have noted that pride is a complex secondary emotion which requires the development of a sense of self and the masking of relevel conceptual distractions.

I am so confident in knowing God for who he is. If anyone tries to take my confidence away.... so be it. They won't get away with it because guilt will play its course. So be it! "Touch not mine anointed and do my prophets no harm." (Psalms 105:15 KJV)

And we know that all things work together for good to them that love God, to them who are the called according to his purpose. Romans 8:28

Is My Black Not Black Enough For You?

Hello, I am a high yellow African-American who's ethnicity or color is labeled as BLACK.

I've been discriminated in crowds, overlooked at times, and called insecure because I wasn't comfortable in the skin that I am in.

Some say I'm beautiful. Other's find their beauty above mine because of their dark colors.

When I look at me, I see their discrimination.

I've been rejected because of my proper language.

I've been used as a door opener for many. Yet, frowned upon because I've been told that I have white in me.

Is my black not black enough for you?

I have curves like the others, but my communication may not be like theirs.

I've been mistreated by my Brothas and Sista's; held down, pushed to the back of the line, and slated for failure for their own selfish gain.

I've been forced to hold my head down so others can hold theirs up.

I've been competed against them all.

I too have been rejected by my white family.

Have you ever heard of Black on black crime?

Been rejected, been cast down?

I don't have ruby red-like skin; I was pushed off to the men. They never protected me; they got rid of me. Was it because of my ancestors' stories?

I have red tones, I have red hair, I have freckles,

I have education,

I have knowledge,

I am wise,

I have integrity,

I have gained pride,

I am, a humble and obedient black woman.

Hello? Is my black not black enough for you.

25 Neither is worshipped with men's hands, as though he needed anything, seeing he giveth to all life, and breath, and all things;

26 And hath made of one blood all nations of men for to dwell on all the face of the earth, and hath determined the times before appointed, and the bounds of their habitation;

(Acts 17:25-26, KJV)

YOU'RE A VERY SPECIAL…IN THE GREAT GOD'S KINGDOM WORLD

You're a very special girly

very special lady

very special woman

In the Great God's Kingdom World

Before you were even thought of you had purpose

To live a life that's full of great big dreams

You are chosen by our Abba Father

He is our daddy and has promises just for you

You are like rubies

You are like diamonds

Sweet smelling flowers

Forming to be pure as gold

That is why it's important that you live this life so full

and go as God plans.

Courageous you are

You are a very special girly

Very special lady

Very special woman in this Great God Kingdom World.

Who knows the plans that He has for you? You just have to wait, trust, and be patient too.

Never worry about your tomorrows.

They are all in his hands, just trust in the master planner, he will always come through.

Love you and He will love you too!

You are a very special girly, very special lady, very special woman in the Great God's Kingdom World.

This was a song that I wrote one day while in the kitchen cooking. I was thinking of my own and the young ladies that had come around my house to hang out with my daughter when writing this song. This song was to encourage all young girls who go through identity crisis in adolescence, who grow and mature into ladies and women.

Just like a cocoon before they turn into butterflies. Just like a bud that blossoms into a flower. We girls grow and mature into ladies; and are married off to become women.

In God's Kingdom, there are steps that leads into maturity. There are lessons that no one wants to rush. Knowing and recognizing that you are special in God's eyes ahead of time will prevent less unnecessary problems.

Please keep yourselves special.

ACKNOWLEDGMENTS

A lady once told me to find myself and learn how to love myself. In the duration of time it really did not come to my mind of her meaning due to emotional scars and unaware of demonic activities that I was once influenced by. I was told to write a book and at the time I didn't know how to start or knew of any inner strength to begin. I struggled with self-confidence and self-assurance for years. I really didn't know my true Identity and self-worth. I was in a whirlwind not knowing my way out. Where was the straight and narrow street? Who was there to guide me? *(Thank you Sharon B.)*

Although, I experienced these challenges that only made me wise and strong; I still needed faith to believe in me. This only came with time. I was challenged by my fears to finish my education, where I was able to read and learn of God's word. I've also gained knowledge through biblical concepts that help me learn of my true identity and purpose. The once angry bitter woman changed into a humble servant.

After, attending a prophetic conference lead by Mark Virkler (author and Minister of God's word), "4 Keys to Hearing God's voice." He said, when meditating through prayer God will minister through writings and hymns (prophetic gifting's). How would you know it is God's voice, it always lines up with his word "the truth?" I began through journaling and somehow it turned into poetry. What an amazing God I serve!

Since, then, I've overcome many fears that once defeated me. I've conquered dreams that I once dreamed. It wasn't until God revealed His promises through the truth in His Word that I no longer ran and stayed still. I could hear again and see again through his revelation power of LOVE.

Love is something everyone needs. If one is unable to love themselves or love others with the love of God, God is the answer. God is love and he loved us so much that he gave the gift of life through Jesus Christ.

It took me three years to complete this book. I struggled so much in my confidence still because of my critics (who only motivated me). It was like a Pictionary experience while writing this book. I went through the emotions of driven through a drama. Don't be surprised that there will be a movie one day. I am so much an overcomer.

I was inspired by other people's stories. My current Pastor, Willie S. Foster, III, Abundant Harvest Church, a dynamic preacher whose gained wisdom and knowledge challenged me in my faith. In my belief, the wife must follow their husband. I had such a struggle with this because I was forced out of my comfort zone. At times, I felt alone but that's how God matured me.

I was inspired by other great writer's and gospel leaders such as Juanita Bynum, Paula White, Joyce Meyer, Dr. Cindy Trimm, Bishop T.D. Jakes, Apostle David E. Taylor, Missionary Rose Smith, Labor of Love Ministries First Lady Hawthorne, Elder Daniel Foster, Elder Benjamin Foster, Prophetess Sun Fanin, and gospel songstress Shana Wilson, Tasha Cobbs, Mary Mary, "Never Wave My Flag", Kirk Franklin "I like Me," and many others. Especially, words from our national leader Barak Obama "Change Can't Happen Without You." I was inspired by women leader's in my church: (Lady Powell, "Love the Skin Your In", Mary E. Foster, "Your Journey to Devine Purpose," Lady Joplin, Women Advanced, Mother Regina Rose Edwards S.W. Jurisdiction #1, A.H.C. Women of Destiny; my country, Michelle Obama, "When they Go Low You Go High,"; my friends, family, and my aunties (they are the greatest).

I was also influenced by the apple of my eye my daughter Janae, a lady of wisdom and much character. I love hard and strong. I love children I love to build them up in their confidence, teaching them how to honor others and themselves. The writing, "You are a very special girly was a song God gave me in my kitchen one day to help me understand our true purpose and identity as a female in "God's Royal Kingdom." I was singing to both of my girl's, while going through a tough time. They both looked at me and laughed.

I didn't know too much about art but I loved it. Did I say my husband is not only an Elder but an anointed musician, "Mr. Bass Man."? I didn't know how to write but only from my heart. I love Maya Angelou's writings the Phenomenal Woman, and Still I Rise! She is an author's whose writing's inspired others to get through life's challenges.

    A special thank you to my dear cousin Tanya Atkins for allowing me to use her painting for the front of my book. The name of her painting is, "Break Out!" She's a very gifted artist whose talent will be known amongst all generations. A thank you to Matthew Holmes for his drawings on the back cover of my book. We will call it, "God Loves Family." He's a visionary artist whose talent will also be made known amongst all generations as well. Thank you to my niece Sonya Miller "S.M. Designs" for your most gifted and talented Graphic Designs.

    I was told that beauty is only skin deep and it is in the eyes of the beholder. Sometimes we must separate ourselves from those who cannot really see. I never really understood this until I could grow up and mature. I wanted to help others to understand their purpose and inner beauty. God beautifies us all through his loving power and character, if you believe.

    No one really has the perfect story or family. Some would say that their imperfections made a life of perfection through their struggle to find Perfection. You are perfect the way you are. Just always find ways of improvement, through excellence. Never be forced to hide your identity behind someone else's. Everyone has a purpose. God has made us all fearfully and wonderfully made. Know your purpose! Never be defeated because, those who believe in God never serves a defeated God. He always Win! I believe God! I am Free!

www.ingramcontent.com/pod-product-compliance
Lightning Source LLC
Chambersburg PA
CBHW060528100426
42743CB00009B/1464